# DRIVEN

# DRIVEN

## Six Incredible Musical Journeys

NICK ROMEO

www.fromthetop.org

Cover photo by Brent Cline

Cover design and page layout by Joanne Robinson

ISBN 9780615511405

This book was drawn from interviews conducted by the author in
2009. Any views or opinions presented in this book are solely those
of the author and do not necessarily represent those of From the Top.

# Author's Acknowledgement

This book would have been impossible without the patience, help and involvement of many people. Thanks to Charles, Greg, Liz, Nadine, Matt, Dasha, and Clifton for generously sharing their time and experiences with me in countless interviews. Thanks also to all of the parents, friends, teachers, and supporters of the book's subjects who took the time to speak with me.

The staff of *From the Top* was also essential to this project. Thanks to Tim, Jerry, Erin, David, Jennifer, and everyone else who gave advice, comments, time, and support to this book.

The book also benefited from the careful readings of friends and family. Thanks to Lia and my parents for all of the support and advice throughout the writing and editing. Finally, Rebecca's editing and support were essential and the project couldn't have happened without her.

# Contents

"WITHOUT MUSIC, LIFE WOULD BE A MISTAKE."
Friedrich Nietzsche

# PRELUDE

In 2006, just after graduating from college, I joined the editorial staff at Carnegie Hall. Since I'd spent most of my time in college playing piano and studying writing, this was a dream job. Not only did I get free tickets to amazing concerts almost every night of the week, I was also able to interview and profile a variety of musicians and hear some of the stories, thoughts, and experiences that motivated their music.

In the fall of 2006, *From the Top* filmed its first season as a PBS television show at Carnegie's Zankel Hall. I'd listened to the show before, but watching a live taping made clear the power of the show's approach. By presenting gifted young musicians in the context of engaging narratives and interviews, the show found a way to do what everyone in the classical music world wanted to do: engage a broad audience.

Through my work at Carnegie Hall, I became interested in telling the stories of young musicians in a longer narrative that could explore certain basic questions: What power does music have in our lives? What drives a young person to work so hard at such a difficult art form? How are traditional notions of classical music being expanded and re-imagined? How can a young classical musician survive in the twenty-first century?

The stories of the six young musicians profiled in this book suggest intriguing answers to these questions. First, we meet several musicians who ignore the restrictive conventions of classical music. They mingle multiple genres and styles of music, engage with audiences in creative and quirky ways, and transform traditional concerts into hybrid events that mix narrative, participation, and a broad range of music. They're evangelists of a vision of classical music as something hip, personal, and capable of appealing to a broad audience.

Next, we take an inside look at the high-stakes world of competition and auditions. We follow two musicians through life-altering moments: the first at the Metropolitan Opera's National Council Auditions, the second through an audition for a seat in the New York Philharmonic.

Finally, we trace the efforts of two young pianists who have transcended difficult circumstances through their music. One young musician travels from a life of homelessness and poverty in the Ukraine to a major American conservatory. The other's vision of classical music becomes enriched by his immersion in the world of gospel music.

Each musician profiled in the book is a *From the Top* alumnus, but all are connected by deeper themes. At a time when classical music seems doomed to irrelevance, they have found ways to perfect and re-invent an old art form and share it with people around the world.

# SECTION 1

## CLASSICAL MUSICIANS CROSSING OVER

# Prodigy Goes Pop

Charles Yang got his first tattoo at a parlor in his hometown of Austin, Texas as an eighteen-year-old high school senior. He hid the tattoo from his parents for almost a week, wearing sweaters and long-sleeved shirts around the house to conceal the intricate design on his upper right arm. Despite his oddly warm clothing – particularly strange in the heat of a Texas spring – his parents didn't suspect anything. Then one Sunday, almost a week after he had gotten the tattoo, Charles and his dad went to church together for the first time in many months. On the drive home, in a confessional mood inspired by the service, Charles pulled off his long-sleeved shirt and showed his dad the tattoo. His dad just laughed. He thought it must be fake. Charles told him it was real and rubbed his arm to prove it. His dad became uneasy. He still wasn't convinced, so he reached over and rubbed the tattoo himself until he finally realized it was permanent. The rest of the ride home was silent. When his mom found out, the sound of her crying filled the house.

Charles' parents wanted him to become a classical violinist. The tattoo was just part of a pattern of rebellion they noticed in his teen years. He'd joined a rock band and become the lead guitarist, he'd grown increasingly social and popular, and he was spending less time in a room by himself practicing violin.

Their concern was understandable. A classical violinist faces ferocious competition and tremendously long odds. Most young classical musicians, with the support of teachers and parents, try to distinguish themselves from others through brute effort in isolation. They sequester themselves in austere practice rooms for long hours and play scales and exercises thousands of times. Sometimes this works, more often it doesn't. But few ever consider the possible value of a different approach.

Charles showed me his first tattoo one afternoon when I met him for pizza a few blocks from the Juilliard School in New York City, where he was a sophomore majoring in violin performance. The tattoo is an intricate black-ink tracing of a traditional Chinese character that means music and happiness. "I thought it was the perfect thing," he explained between bites, pulling up the sleeve of his T-shirt to display the ancient calligraphy.

In frayed blue jeans, a tight white T-shirt, and tinted sunglasses, Charles looked more like a grungy rock guitarist than a budding classical virtuoso. He was even carrying a guitar, not a violin, when we met for pizza. The more time I spent with Charles, the more I started to think that what his parents saw as a dangerous rebellious streak – the tattoos, the rock music, the socializing – was precisely what might enable him to succeed.

Charles got his second tattoo late in his senior year of high school. After his parents' reaction to the first one, he knew they wouldn't approve of a second – that was sort of the point. "I'd had a fight with my dad, plus I was just bored," he said. His parents certainly weren't pleased, but they were less upset than the first time. The second tattoo is a small Chinese dragon on his upper left arm; the dragon is the animal of his birth year, 1988.

He got his third and last tattoo at a parlor in Greenwich Village during his first year at Juilliard. Inspired by the Lynyrd Skynyrd song "Free Bird," it is an image of a bird with wings spread wide across the muscles of Charles' upper back. By this point, his parents had, in his words, "pretty much given up. Now they just tease me about it."

In their mixture of tradition and rebellion – ancient Chinese symbols and modern American rock – Charles' tattoos seemed to mirror a larger quality in his personality and his musical endeavors: he's a rock guitarist and self-proclaimed "Asian cowboy," a lover of good barbeque, high school football, and all things Texan, but he's also a brilliant classical violinist, a lover of Brahms and Paganini and a virtuoso capable of thriving in the country's most elite musical conservatory. This rare mixture of elements is not a set of schizophrenic contradictions so much as the various outpourings of a single exuberant personality; his versatility is not a shortcoming, it's his chief attraction.

This probably sounds obvious until you consider that two of the main environments in which Charles has spent time – an elite conservatory and a traditional Chinese household – tend to discourage departures from the orthodoxy that says a classical musician ought to spend a majority of his time and effort playing classical music. As I got to know a variety of young musicians at Juilliard and other conservatories while reporting this book, I realized just how unconventional Charles is in light of his current surroundings and his background.

Charles' exposure to classical music began in the womb. His mom is a violinist who trained at China's prestigious Shanghai Conservatory and got a job playing in the Austin Symphony when she and her husband moved to America. The night before he was born, the symphony had a performance of Max Bruch's Violin Concerto, a staple of the Romantic repertoire. When Charles played the piece just over a decade later, it was unusually easy for him. His mom, only partly joking, told him it was the first piece he ever played.

But when Charles actually began to play his first pieces on the violin, it was hardly a smooth or idyllic experience. "I hated it," he recalled. "I was three years old when my mom shoved a violin in my hands, you know, it's like the Asian rule, and I remember hating it and thinking, 'Man, it doesn't even sound good.'"

In addition to her symphony job, his mom also had a private studio of violin students, the youngest of whom, for a time, was Charles. At his first recital, when he was four, he turned and faced the corner while he played: "My ass was facing the audience the whole time." To get him to practice, his parents would bribe him with M&Ms and other small treats. Even so, it was a struggle: "Past thirty minutes I'd always cry and shout, 'Why do I have to do more?'"

Ages three to five were the hardest. Charles' dad would sit with him and supervise his practice every day. "If he hadn't done that, I'd probably be in a different field right now." Mandating and supervising a daily practice session is a delicate parental decision. If a young child has total freedom he or she may drift away from music entirely and regret that they weren't compelled to master an instrument during crucial early years. Yet overly strict requirements and demands can easily inspire a negative reaction; instead of being a source of enjoyment and beauty, music becomes clouded with pressure and anxiety and feels like a burden or chore.

Despite his vocal objections at the time, Charles is one of the lucky few who got the best of both worlds: his early practicing gave him a firm foundation without destroying his love of music. He now feels, "very grateful that they forced me to play." When he was five, he started to notice the skill of some of his mom's older violin students. "I was basically just jealous of her better students, so I started to practice harder to compete, to get attention."

But while success as a violinist could get him the attention of his parents, his peers couldn't have cared less. "No one gave a shit about classical in grade school, it was always sports, sports, sports." When people did talk about music they talked about popular music – Britney Spears, The Spice Girls, Green Day. One day in the second grade, Charles added his two cents to a playground chat about music. He'd been listening to the violinist Pinchas Zukerman at home, and while Zukerman is certainly famous in the classical world, he doesn't exactly give second-grader credibility on the playground. When Charles excitedly told a group of friends how cool "Pinky Zukerman" was, their eyebrows raised and their faces sneered. "They were like 'What? Who? You're stupid!'" They teased him for weeks. After that he kept his classical music name dropping to a minimum.

While Charles was practicing violin, almost everyone else was playing soccer. Soccer was huge. He started to feel embarrassed about the violin and soon he joined a youth soccer team. He even made it to a select squad of the best players only to have to quit to allow more time for violin practice. "It killed me, the day I had to quit. Music kind of killed my childhood. I was always practicing."

Many highly gifted musicians have blissful early years; their talent wins them attention and praise and they coast easily into their adolescence before starting to feel the pressure of competition and the difficulty of achieving excellence on their instrument. Charles' trajectory seemed to have been the opposite; his early years were a struggle and only later did he start to find acceptance, acclaim, and a real love for music.

By the time he was ten, his talent and hard work started to pay off. He had already surpassed the older students in his mom's violin studio whom he used to envy and his parents sent him to the famous performing arts camp in Interlochen, Michigan. He spent four summer weeks living in a log cabin in the woods, surrounded by other kids who loved and played classical music. It was the first time he felt proud of what he did. It was also the first time he saw a naked woman. He was wandering through an art building one afternoon when he glimpsed a nude model posing for an art class. If only he were an art student!

That summer was a great musical success. Charles demonstrated a much greater talent than he or his parents had realized. People started to use the word prodigy. His parents hadn't thought music would be a career before that summer; it was an important part of the upbringing they wanted him to have and something they hoped he'd continue throughout his life, but it wasn't what they considered a viable career. During that first summer at Interlochen, he won the concerto competition, besting some of the most gifted musicians from around the country. After he won the competition again the next summer, performing via live web-cam for an audience of thousands of viewers, the camp's president called Charles' parents to congratulate them and tell them how gifted he thought Charles was. What had seemed like a serious hobby began to look like a destined career.

After Interlochen, Charles began studying with other teachers besides his mom. His performing career also began to accelerate. A Chinese friend of his mom's with political connections arranged for him to perform at a huge auditorium in Shenzhen, China. The event was billed as "An Evening with Charles Yang." He played a violin concerto by J.S. Bach, but he also sang the standards "On Top of Old Smokey" and "Red River" to appeal to the audience's love of all things American. It was the first of many concerts he would play that mixed classical and non-classical music.

The next year, Charles toured Europe, missing several weeks of school and playing at a number of important venues. It was a blur of castles and concert halls, airports, and sightseeing. One memorable concert took place in a duke's mansion in Germany. "My friends were like 'Hey man, you missed some great soccer games, where'd you go?' I said, 'Well, I had to play for a duke in Germany.' They thought it was so cool." By the time he got to high school just over a year later, the story of the duke had blossomed into the rumor that Charles had played a private concert and had tea with the Queen of England.

In early high school, he started to feel his music was no longer an obstacle to social acceptance. Part of the change was his friends' maturity, but Charles had also begun to enjoy non-classical music. His friends loved his playing and suddenly it seemed that almost everyone was his friend. He'd often bring an old beat-up violin to campfire parties and jam on fiddle music and bluegrass or just take requests. "People were always asking for *Titanic*. 'Dude, play the theme from *Titanic!*'"

He also began to be known for things besides music. In a biology class his sophomore year, the students were dissecting a pig when Charles and a few friends had the kind of great idea only fifteen year-old boys have. They discreetly removed their pig's eyes, cut off its testicles, and placed the testicles in the eye sockets. When the teacher, on whom all the boys had a crush, came around to inspect their progress, she shrieked with horror and ran from the room.

He was the class clown in virtually all of his classes throughout high school and his antics often landed him in the principal's office. But even the principal couldn't resist Charles' charms. They got along so well (and saw each other so often) that by Charles' senior year he was teaching the principal to play the guitar. Given a little more time, they probably would have kicked back with a beer.

The Queen of England rumor was a good start, but Charles' musical celebrity got a more tangible boost when he was featured on an Austin taping and national broadcast of the radio version of *From the Top*. "Basically anything related to the media or fame, people think is awesome, so I got kids coming up to me like 'Dude, my mom and I were driving and heard you on the radio!'" What hooked his friends was that the show wasn't just about Charles' music, it was also about Charles. He began by playing the Spanish composer Pablo de Sarasate's dazzling showpiece *Zigeunerweisen* ("Gypsy Airs"). The work has been a classic of the virtuoso repertoire ever since Sarasate himself played it throughout Europe in the nineteenth century. After the performance he told host Christopher O'Riley that violin, like Coca Cola, was so addictive that he couldn't put it down. They also talked about his small part in the movie *Spy Kids 2* (his dad had a friend who got him the part, which consists of him saying the word 'hello' in Chinese) and joked about the difficulties of having your mom as a teacher. "A bunch of my friends knew nothing about classical music, but they liked the interactions, that it was about me. If it was just a normal recital with no talking, it wouldn't attract people."

At sixteen, Charles began entering classical competitions in Texas and around the country. He won almost every one of them. After one victory, he persuaded his mom to buy him his first guitar. He'd always been drawn to the instrument, but his parents would never agree to buy him one – they wanted him to focus on the violin. Even now, when Charles is home from Juilliard and jamming or performing with his rock band, his parents dismiss it as "just for fun." As soon as he got his first guitar he fell in love with it, even though it was just a cheap $99.00 instrument: "I never will sell that first one, not that anybody would want it anyway." He quickly taught himself how to play, instinctively mastering chord progressions and melodies. Perfect pitch – the ability to identify and play any note he hears – and a perfect memory for music didn't hurt his learning curve.

Soon he was jamming regularly with the group that would become his band, Charlie Railroad. His parents weren't pleased: "They'd get so upset when I'd jam and go to practice with the band. They always said 'Stop wasting time, you need to practice more violin.'" Charles was determined not to sacrifice either classical or rock, he saw them as different but equally vital types of expression. Even at Juilliard, a bastion of all things classical, he retains a strong love for both types of music. "If there's one thing I want to do in my life," he told me, "it's to merge classical and popular music."

As Charlie Railroad began performing at different venues and live music festivals around Texas, that's exactly what he started to do. The band would play a set, mostly covers of classic rock songs and some of their own compositions, and then during the breaks between sets Charles would take out his violin and play a classical showpiece, often a Paganini Caprice or something similarly virtuosic. The crowds loved it and soon a tradition was established: a set of rock followed by a bit of classical wizardry.

He was still excelling on the violin, winning competitions and attending elite music festivals like the Aspen Music Festival in Colorado (where he won the concerto competition). But his playing had become just one part of a more balanced life. It was no longer an isolating burden but a way to have fun and bring people together. At campfire parties – think teenagers, fire, and beer – he became legendary for his ability to play virtually any song people requested. Music just stuck in his head; if he heard a song once he could play it back perfectly. And if he had never heard a song that someone requested, they would whistle its melody and Charles would play it back, complete with harmony and improvised embellishments. He was still the kid who thought "Pinky" Zukerman was so cool, but now he not only knew the music the other kids liked, he could even play it for them. During his senior year he became the first Asian person in the school's history to be voted homecoming prince, and his pranks and jokes continued to amuse the school. One day in his senior year, he shocked and delighted a large crowd by standing in the central courtyard of the school and serenading an elderly female teacher while doing a striptease. His frequent visits to the principal's office helped the principal's guitar skills.

He also found a strong supporter in *From the Top*. After a second appearance on the radio show and performances at private events *From the Top* organized (including visiting the Britney Spears Performing Arts Camp for underprivileged kids), Charles was chosen to appear on the first season of the public television version of the show filmed live at Carnegie Hall. A *From the Top* film crew flew to Austin and shot footage of Charles jamming with his band, cruising the city streets in his red Mustang, and eating his mom's Chinese cooking with his friends. They also filmed a comic sequence featuring Charles roaming around the city asking people on the streets if they knew it was Charles Yang Day. (After playing at a city council meeting, the mayor had actually named a day for Charles.) In the film sequence, we see Charles going from person to person, asking things like, "How are you celebrating Charles Yang Day?" or exclaiming with mock horror, "You don't know about Charles Yang Day?!?" Finally, he makes it to the mayor and requests that, at the very least, the schools and banks be closed in his honor.

His appearance on the television show was a huge success. He played a dashing showpiece by the Italian composer Monti, chatted and joked with host Christopher O'Riley, and watched the background montage the crew had filmed in Austin. Another sequence in the montage shows Charles and a few friends in his living room. His mom insists on playing a DVD of Charles performing the last movement of Tchaikovsky's violin concerto with an orchestra at the Aspen Music Festival. Despite a few mumbled protests from Charles, she plays the video. The camera shows the video of Charles playing for a few seconds and then pans to the face of a friend, whose mouth has literally dropped open with astonishment. "That's incredible," he murmurs.

Charles' friends, family, and teachers all loved the *From the Top* episode. And so did people he'd never met. For months afterward he got a steady stream of messages and friend requests on Facebook from people who had seen the show. Glenn Dicterow, the concertmaster of the New York Philharmonic and Charles' teacher at Juilliard, saw the episode before meeting Charles; he still jokes with him about Charles Yang Day. The producer of the MTV show *Unplugged* also saw the episode and approached Charles with an offer to host a TV show for kids about music on Nickelodeon. Charles flew to New York to meet with the producer and discuss the possibilities, but in the meantime he had been accepted to Dicterow's violin studio at Juilliard. As tempting as potential TV stardom was, he decided that since this chance had come along, others would too. He accepted Juilliard's offer and moved to New York City.

Another chance did come along, though not until halfway through Charles' sophomore year at Juilliard. Early in the year he was starting to get worried; he hadn't played any major concerts lately and he was thinking that maybe he ought to practice orchestral excerpts for symphony auditions. But he still wanted to be a crossover artist, a pioneer who could hop between classical and popular music and bring fresh ideas to fans of both genres. "The extremes scare me," he told me one day at Juilliard. "On the one hand, there's just playing in an orchestra or just being a classical soloist. There are thousands of awesome classical violinists out there, all trying to do the same thing. I just wonder how many different recordings of a given classical piece the world needs. But I don't think I could play only rock 'n roll either. Part of me just loves classical too much."

An unprecedented number of polished and technically flawless classical musicians have come of age just as live audiences are dwindling and CD sales have sharply declined. Many of these young musicians were practicing in the rooms all around us on Juilliard's fourth floor. For this new generation of classical musicians to focus exclusively on the traditional repertoire assumes that a general audience will find a meaningful difference between incredibly subtle expressive distinctions. Twenty concert violinists may all shape a given phrase in a given piece with minutely different areas of emphasis and concepts of style, but very few people will want to own all twenty recordings of the piece. For most people, the choice is not between different classical artists; it's between classical music and popular forms of music. Charles seemed to have grasped this reality in a way few classical musicians have. Rather than maintain an insular focus and simply assume an audience for classical music will always exist, he wants to actively create that audience, and to persuade and seduce others into enjoying a type of music as passionately as he does.

This attitude manifests itself even in Charles' practicing habits at Juilliard. While other students tend to stay isolated in their practice rooms, Charles circulates between rooms, telling a joke in one, playing a duet in another, jamming on the blues in a third. If you spend any time with Charles at Juilliard, it quickly becomes clear that, in the words of one student, "Everyone loves Charles." He can't seem to walk down a hallway without being rubbed on the head, patted on the arm, given a high-five, or told that it's been too long since they hung out. He's like a combination of holy relic and team mascot – people either want to touch him or cheer him on.

But despite his popularity and unusual practice routine, by his sophomore year at Juilliard he was starting to feel too caught up in the daily grind. Without performances and audiences to connect with, it was easy to forget what the goal of practicing a thousand tiny details really was. Every day seemed monotonously similar to every other day: eat, practice, eat, practice, sleep, and then repeat.

His luck changed midway through the year. Since late high school, Charles had taught a small number of violin students in Texas. The mother of one of his students was the sister of a powerful music agent in Taiwan. She told him about Charles and he asked Charles to send him some recordings. Charles sent off the footage of

his *From the Top* television appearance and his Tchaikovsky performance at Aspen, not expecting anything to come of it. A few weeks
later he was offered an all-expenses-paid trip to Taiwan, where he
was to meet and play for some of the most powerful music agents
and producers in the country.

Two weeks before the trip to Taiwan, I met Charles in the Juilliard lobby and we walked over to an apartment building a few
blocks away for a lesson with Glenn Dicterow. Charles is one of
Dicterow's biggest fans, and the feeling seems to be mutual. On the
elevator ride up to his apartment, a gorgeous unit on the 26th floor
of a luxury building, Charles said Dicterow "can still shred like no
other." As soon as I heard Dicterow pick up his violin to demonstrate
something, I knew exactly what Charles meant. Even on the fastest
and most difficult passages, his technique and intonation were perfect. Intonation is one of the many difficulties a violinist faces. As
long as a piano is properly tuned, anyone can play with perfect intonation. But a violinist, like other string players, must place his finger
in exactly the right spot on a string to produce a given note and he
does not have the assistance of discrete units called keys to help him.
Playing with good intonation takes years to master and playing with
perfect intonation is something few people ever do. Dicterow's ability to "shred like no other" meant he could play extremely rapidly
with flawless intonation.

Before the lesson, Charles told me Dicterow was "like a teenager," which for Charles is high praise. Dicterow lacked any of the
formality you might expect from an esteemed Juilliard professor.
To help Charles evoke the elusive charm of the Kreisler showpiece
he was working on, Dicterow sang certain phrases in a husky baritone voice, played them with brilliant precision on the violin, offered
similes and descriptions to convey the spirit of the music, and finally
put on an old LP recording of the piece by the legendary violinist
Zino Francescatti.

"It's sort of a ghostly thing, this melody," Dicterow explained. "It
has to throb, even in the silences. It has to have that early twentieth
century panache. Kreisler learned how to play in cafes. It's not so
driven, like a railroad engine; it has to have charm, it's Viennese."

Charles wiggled his eyebrows suggestively. "Like the Viennese
women," he said.

Dicterow smiled. "I don't know about that Charles."

"Me neither, but I hope to find out some day."

Dicterow demonstrated passages or techniques and then Charles would play them, trying to get the bow to bounce off the strings more freely or to produce a different degree of vibration on a given note. Sometimes they would trade violins, but it was clear that each was more accustomed to his own instrument. Charles plays an 1826 violin built in the workshop of the French craftsman Charles Gane. At $75,000, it was a relative bargain (the famed Stradivarius violins often cost over a million dollars, but his parents still took out a second mortgage to afford it.) By the end of the lesson, the combination of talking, trading, joking, listening, and playing seemed to have given Charles a new understanding of the piece.

"He's incredible," Dicterow told me later. "He learns and memorizes so quickly, sometimes my job is just making him slow down. When you have so much talent it is important to really focus on the basic things, the foundation." Dicterow has taught at Juilliard since the late 1980s, but Charles has something he hardly ever sees in classical musicians. "It's very rare, that magnetic star quality. It's so hard for anyone to have a thriving career these days – I think it is a good thing for Charles to explore his options, one of which may be breaking out into the world of pop and bringing the violin with him, bringing it to other people who wouldn't otherwise hear the violin."

♪ ♪ ♪

Charles knew he was going to meet influential people in Taiwan, but the details were hazy. All he knew was that his student's mom's brother, a man named Ray, was flying him to Taiwan so he could meet with and play for some of the country's most powerful music agents. He also knew they had high hopes for him based on his sample DVD. "They want to make me the Justin Timberlake of Asia," he told me. If the visit went well, he might have to choose between finishing his degree at Juilliard and starting a career in Asia.

Charles flew into Taipei, the capital of Taiwan, on a Sunday night. Ray met him at the airport in his BMW. At first, Ray was formal and reserved. By the end of the week's visit they were drinking together, smoking Cuban cigars and talking like old friends. But their first meeting was somewhat restrained. On the drive home, they stopped at what's known as a night-market: a nocturnal festival or market with a variety of stalls, booths, and merchants tucked into some of the city's innumerable alleys. Ray treated Charles to stinky tofu – "smells so bad, but tastes so good" and authentic bubble tea. The BMW had been a bit of a surprise, and Ray's apartment, a huge, luxurious dwelling near the top of a towering building, was also unexpected. Charles savored the view of the unknown city and the Danshui River and then collapsed into bed, exhausted from the flight.

The next morning, Ray took him to his office and explained that his business involved public relations for car companies. This was a bigger surprise than the BMW or the apartment, though both started to make more sense now. He thought Ray was a music agent, not a businessman. He started to get worried and wonder what exactly he was doing there. He played a few pieces for Ray's employees and Ray asked them if they thought he would be a star. They applauded their approval. Then he played for a friend of Ray's who was an agent. The man seemed uninterested, telling Ray that, at twenty, Charles was already too old to be marketable. The trip was starting to seem like a bad idea.

The next day Charles played for another powerful agent who came to Ray's office. Charles played a classical piece – Ravel's *Tzigane* – but he spiced it up with blues licks and improvisation. The agent loved it. He wanted to record and distribute a live album. He also gauged Charles' marketability by interviewing him. "It's Asia, I mean so many people there can play the violin like it's a toy, just technically perfect, so they want you to have a personality too," Charles said. Ten thousand hours in a practice room might make you technically perfect, but sometimes a quick wit or the right smile is the key factor in a decisive moment. Charles' usual charisma quickly asserted itself and the agent left the meeting smitten, promising to be in touch.

Next he and Ray drove to Sony's corporate headquarters in a huge building in Taipei's business district. Seeing how many connections Ray had, Charles was starting to worry less. Ray arranged for Charles to play for the general manager of Sony Taiwan, a talent impresario who has helped launch many of Asia's musical pop superstars. He was ushered into a plush, private room in Sony Taiwan's corporate offices. "It was like the knights of the round table – a room with a huge oval table, or like those scenes in CIA movies where they sit in the decision room and the walls turn into projection screens and people start moving things around with their hands," Charles said. He played a classical piece, Vieuxtemps' variations on "Yankee Doodle Dandy," and then Ray found him a guitar and he played one of his own compositions, a song called "Fire" with a classic rock sound. He told Ray that Charles was definitely marketable, both as a classical or a crossover artist.

For dinner that night they went to the apartment of one of Taiwan's most famous photographers, an eighty-year-old man named Koh who has photographed Miles Davis, Andy Warhol, and hundreds of Taiwanese artists and celebrities. As the red wine flowed and the dinner and conversation stretched into the night, any lingering doubts Charles had melted away.

Ray arranged a concert for potential sponsors on Friday. On Wednesday he rehearsed with a pianist Ray found to accompany him. Charles thought she was beautiful, but she couldn't play the difficult music. "I'm acting like it's no big deal, but inside I'm freaked, like this will blow my chances Friday," he said. Despite his worries, he couldn't find a graceful way to tell her to learn the music.

That night Ray took him to dinner at a famous Japanese restaurant with a few of his friends: a designer, a theater agent, and a wine importer. Ray booked a private V.I.P. room and the waitresses were not only beautiful but also very flirtatious. "They're treating me like a friend. 'Hodale' means cheers, and when you hear it you're supposed to drink, so every two seconds I'm hearing 'hodale', 'hodale.'" Course after course of Japanese food and bottle after bottle of expensive wine and champagne kept emerging from the kitchen. During one course, perhaps in cosmic revenge for his high school prank, Charles had to eat a Taiwanese delicacy: chicken testicles. "I didn't even know chickens had testicles. I bit into one and all these juices came out and I said, 'I'm not touching the other one.' They all cracked up." After a few more 'hodales,' the group insisted he play something on the violin. He'd never played classical music drunk before, but he launched into a few Paganini caprices and they felt effortless. The group started requesting songs and they were amazed by his capacity to play perfectly what he'd heard only once. They'd whistle something and he'd play it back, however long or complicated, with melody and often harmony. Soon the waitresses, who seemed even more beautiful than before, were chiming in with requests. The party lasted well into the night.

The next morning Ray had arranged for Charles to do a radio interview on one of Taipei's classical music radio stations. Mandarin is Charles' third language after Cantonese and English, so he was a little nervous about giving an interview in Mandarin while hung-over, but he understood all the questions and kept his answers simple and clear. He also played some classical and blues violin and soon the radio host had him playing the same whistle-and-playback game as the night before, only this time it was for a live radio audience of hundreds of thousands. He played snippets of the Brahms, Tchaikovsky, and Mendelssohn violin concertos, the theme from *The Lion King*, and popular Taiwanese songs – basically whatever was whistled or requested.

Later that day he had a second rehearsal for Friday's concert. Ray had noticed Charles' discomfort with the pianist the day before and quickly booked an accompanist Charles later learned was literally the most expensive accompanist in Taiwan. She regularly played for Andrea Bocelli and other musical celebrities. Not surprisingly, the rehearsal was a success. "She was incredible, I mean she followed me perfectly, every slight ritard or acceleration," Charles said.

Dinner that night was another confirmation of Ray's seemingly infinite network of powerful and influential friends. At a fancy Japanese restaurant, they dined with the president of Ford Motors in Taiwan. On the way home, Ray offered to let Charles drive a brand-new Audi. "I'm terrified, this is an $80,000 car in crazy Asian traffic, but I couldn't resist," he said. They got home with both car and passengers unscathed and Charles collapsed into bed.

The next day was his last in Taiwan. He'd squeezed a terrific number of meetings into a few short days, and a growing stack of business cards confirmed all the contacts he'd made. His trust in Ray was growing quickly, and when Ray asked Charles if he wanted him as an agent, Charles accepted the offer.

In the morning, they met again with the agent who had said Charles was already too old. Somehow, he had gotten word of Charles' meeting with Sony and other agents and he'd suddenly reconsidered. They met at a cafe the agent had just bought and he told

Charles and Ray he was planning on converting it into a club featuring live classical music. He wanted Charles to play there in June or July. Another business card joined the stack.

That night Charles performed for potential sponsors. Ray rented a restaurant with a stage and the heads of major corporations like Ford and Acer computers, as well as musical agents and even a famous Asian actor, were gathered at tables to enjoy the music. In jeans and jacket, Charles mingled with the crowd for a little while before playing a concert that mixed classical, blues, and rock. The audience loved it. Soon they were calling out and humming requests. After the music came more mingling and drinking and a few hours later, Charles, Ray, and a few friends puffed Cuban cigars and shared rare wines while listening to old classical records at a friend's office. They stayed out until 6 A.M. and as Charles was leaving, the man whose office they were in asked him what year he was born. Charles told him and the man came back and handed him a bottle of French wine from 1988 as a gift.

There was no time to sleep before his return flight. He felt exhausted but happy – the trip had been a great experience. And while he had played his classical repertoire beautifully, his ability to chat and drink and mingle, and his excitement about a variety of musical genres had been far more important than the mere perfection of his playing. He had made clear a fundamental value that distinguishes him from many musicians: he sees music not as a way to display his own greatness and difference from others, but as a way to connect with others, to close the space between people.

One night just before he left for his Taiwan trip, I sat in on a jam session with Charles and a few of his friends on the fourth floor of the Juilliard School. It was the kind of evening Charles tends to create wherever he is – at a campfire party in Texas, a swanky club in Taiwan, or a cramped practice room at Juilliard. As we walked into the school, Charles stopped to chat with a security guard. Charles was selling him a guitar and they swapped details and bargained over the price.

On the fourth floor we met Charles' friend Peter and found a room. Charles plugged his guitar into a small amp, Peter took the piano, and they launched into a slow blues. Soon they transitioned into "Let It Be" and then "Georgia on My Mind." Even in a practice room without a crowd, Charles' rock star quality is irrepressible. He moves his head in rhythm with the beat, sways his hips and squeezes his eyes shut as he improvises a guitar lick or croons out the chorus of a song. Pretty soon other students started to drift in from neighboring practice rooms. A young violinist named Maria walked in and Charles, without missing a beat, began improvising lyrics in her honor "ooo Maria, baby you look so fine/ you got a belt around your waist/ why not take it off?" Now Maria's name inspired a segue into Bernstein's "Maria" From *West Side Story*. The rest of the night continued in the same vein – they jumped from Beethoven to the Beatles, Chopin to Pink Floyd, Handel to Gloria Gaynor.

After a few sets, Charles put down his guitar and picked up his violin, the dozens of tiny scratches and nicks in the surface of the dark cherry-wood a visible testimony to his years of passionate playing. It seemed almost as if the violin were no longer a piece of finely carved wood, but had become an organic extension of his body, a kind of extra limb. The crowd swelled with other students lured by the rare sounds emanating from the practice room and the small space heated up. Charles stripped down to his usual white T-shirt and I caught a glimpse of his first tattoo – the ancient character for music and happiness – and thought it was a more perfect symbol than anyone has yet realized.

*Charles already had a violin
in his hands by the age of three*

*Charles on From the Top (left at age fourteen and right at eighteen)*

*At his Juilliard recital (left) and
with one of his current bands
"Sultans of Sweat" (above)*

photo credit: Arthur Moeller

photo credit: Brent Cline

# Piano 2.0

During his second year as an undergraduate at Juilliard, pianist Greg Anderson noticed something strange about himself and his classmates. They didn't enjoy going to classical concerts and recitals. Greg was constantly falling asleep at recitals. It felt strange to admit it, but he found many of the recitals kind of boring. He went to see the drama students' plays and noticed other drama students were thrilled to see their peers' work. Why wasn't the same true of music students? How can you make people excited about classical music?

These are questions Greg has spent the last decade trying to answer. He felt that if even classical musicians were less than excited about going to classical concerts, then the general public would continue to yawn their way through concerts or avoid them entirely. Plays and drama had a natural advantage over classical music: people died, fought, fell in love. In other words, the content was blatantly relevant to real life. But he knew music can also speak directly to fundamental human concerns, even if it does so in a different language.

Part of the problem was that by the time he started studying at Juilliard, he could only listen critically. "Going to recitals became very frustrating. I'd hear some gorgeous bit of Mozart and be thinking 'that slur could have been more graceful,' or 'their tone isn't transparent enough,'" he recalled. Around the same time that Greg was thinking about how to make recitals more exciting, he started playing duets with a pianist and Juilliard classmate named Elizabeth Joy Roe. They were friends before they were musical partners – they watched Harry Potter movies together, they went out to eat Chinese food – and the playfulness of their friendship naturally carried over to their musical endeavors. They felt an instant musical chemistry and decided to organize a recital of music for piano duo. For their first public concert, they took an unusually creative approach. They made a different poster for every piece they were performing – they drew a skeleton for Saint-Saëns' "Danse Macabre," found an ornate Germanic script to advertise a piece by Brahms – and hung them all over Juilliard. They also created original narration to accompany their performance of *The Carnival of the Animals* and interspersed the music with spoken narrative. The result was a great success. The crowd laughed and cheered throughout the recital, and no one fell asleep.

I first met Greg and Liz almost a decade later. It was a spring day in New Haven, Connecticut, where Greg was pursuing a doctorate in Piano Performance at Yale. "We need batteries, duct tape, and a flashlight," Greg said. We were walking to a thrift store in downtown New Haven to search for supplies. In a few hours, Greg and Liz were shooting a music video for their paraphrase of the Bee Gees song "Stayin' Alive." "Are we gonna be destroying anything in slow motion?" Liz asked in a serious voice. "We can bring that lamp I don't want," Greg said.

At the New Haven Salvation Army they fanned out and searched the aisles for flared jeans, bell bottoms, tapered shirts with pointed collars, anything reminiscent of the 1970's. Greg found a marigold shirt with a brown floral pattern and a pointed collar. He made for the register. "I haven't seen one of these in a long time," the cashier said as he counted out change.

Greg and Liz played together as Anderson & Roe throughout both undergraduate and masters' degrees at Juilliard, and since early 2007 they have created over a dozen music videos that give visual and dramatic dimensions to various compositions for piano duo. Collectively, their videos have been viewed well over a million times on YouTube, which makes them one of the most popular piano duos in the world.

Anderson & Roe's musical paraphrases exhibit many of the traits Franz Liszt developed in his famous paraphrases of Italian opera in

the nineteenth century: they're virtuosic and often playful trans-
formations of familiar material into novel forms and styles. While
the Bee Gees might seem an unlikely source of material for classi-
cally trained pianists, Greg saw historical continuity in the choice:
"Saint-Saëns took the can-can, a popular contemporary dance song,
and slowed it down for his 'Carnival of the Animals.' We wanted to
pick something that people would recognize as a dance song, and
'Stayin' Alive' is certainly that." As a nod to Saint-Saëns they titled
their rendition "Turtle Stayin' Alive." They had recorded the audio
for the video months ago. That night they were hosting and filming
what amounted to a dance party to match the music.

After they left the Salvation Army, Greg and Liz returned to
Greg's apartment and watched a YouTube clip from *Saturday Night
Fever* in which a young John Travolta struts down the street eating
pizza, then ducks into a dance club and displays astounding pel-
vic mobility while dancing to "Stayin' Alive." They took notes and
brainstormed as they watched. "I like rows of people on the sides.
The problem is I can't dance like that. Also, we don't have a glowing
floor," said Greg. Next they watched a music video by the indie band
Broken Social Scene. It showed a bunch of young people partying
in a house; the dancing was decidedly easier to imitate than John
Travolta's, the visual esthetic was low-tech and black-and-white.

After a quick dinner of stir fry tofu and cold sesame noodles, they
were ready to go. Greg changed into a pair of shiny red shoes, flared
bell bottoms, and the marigold shirt from the Salvation Army. Liz
wore a black and brown checked shirt, platform shoes, and high-
waisted black pants. They drove to an apartment a friend had offered for the shoot and cleared out the furniture. Their supplies for
the evening were crammed into a cardboard box: orange juice, beer,
seltzer water, batteries, a flashlight, two five-dollar disco balls from
Target, a Canon HV30 video camera, and a bottle of vodka. Soon
friends recruited for dancing skills or enthusiasm – mostly the latter
– started to trickle in and mix drinks, as a stream of disco hits blasted
from the speakers. Greg set up the camera, coached the people on
the general idea of the video – "Basically it's just people dancing in a
room" – and maneuvered the disco balls and flashlight to create the
desired swirl of lights on the apartment's green walls. As the alcohol

made its way from bottles into bloodstreams, the dancing became wilder. By midnight they had filmed over three hours of footage for a video that would be just under three minutes long.

One of their most popular videos re-imagines Astor Piazzolla's "Libertango." The video opens in a college classroom as a professorial voice drones on about Newton's Laws governing force and attraction between bodies. Dressed as college students, Greg and Liz sit yawning and making flirtatious eyes at each other. Soon the video cuts to a shot of Liz draped suggestively over a grand piano on an empty stage. Then Greg appears, dressed in tight black leather, and begins to play. As he plays, Liz manually dampens the strings inside the piano's sound-box. The effect is two-fold: the percussive timbre suggests the sound of a tango band, while Liz's position evokes the intimacy of the dance.

"We tried to imitate the danger and friction of tango. Are they gonna trip over each other? Elements of the dance are literally transcribed into the music," Greg said, describing the video. Their performance also emphasizes the sensuality of the dance; they exchange sultry gazes at the piano bench, fling their heads back in ecstasy after hitting certain chords and tangle and intertwine their arms. The video ends back in the classroom with Greg startling awake as the dry voice of the physics professor finishes a sentence, so the bulk of the video seems like a Dionysian daydream during a dull lecture. Every aspect of the rendition – their arrangement, performance, attire, and the miniature narrative frame – enhances the essential character of Piazzolla's music.

♩ ♩ ♩

Arrangements and compositions for piano duo began to proliferate in the early nineteenth century. By that time, the instrument had expanded in length to the point that a single piano could accommodate two people. The expansion in size was driven in part by the demand for precisely this capacity and in part by the ambitious compositions of Beethoven and other composers that exhausted the range of existing pianos and drove the instrument closer to its current size. Before recording technology brought instant access to musical entertainment, the easiest and often only way to enjoy music was by making it yourself or attending gatherings at which others played.

But the domestic origins of the genre generated a repertoire of predominantly simple and unchallenging music that could provide an evening of entertainment to the largest number of households.

"Music for one-piano, four-hands tends to be very domestic and feminine," said Greg. "Think of two pigtailed sisters and an audience of grandmothers muttering, 'Oh, so precious, they are playing on the recital!' All we could think of was little girls, it was so lame. So we said, 'Let's make it concert worthy.' A couple of pieces stood out, and we just had to compose the rest," Greg said. The associations Greg had with the piano duo are a microcosm of the impressions many people have of classical music in general: quaint, gentle, a realm of grandmothers and sleepiness. Greg and Liz take an iconoclastic pleasure in smashing through the stereotype of classical music as a tame and harmless anachronism. They want audiences to have powerful, visceral reactions to their music. After hearing their exuberantly virtuosic take on Strauss' "Blue Danube" waltz at a concert in Oregon, one woman in the audience leapt to her feet and shouted, "Now that's a waltz!"

This is exactly the reaction they want to provoke. Greg and Liz consider many aspects of classical concert etiquette not just arbitrary, but actively destructive. Prohibitions against spontaneous applause, casual attire, and talking are all relatively recent phenomena that tend to imbue classical music with an almost holy aura of seriousness and high purpose. Funny or playful music is received with solemn silence or stern nods of approval. "People treat Mozart like his music was delivered to the hands of God, but it was delivered to the commoners of Vienna. They would laugh aloud during performances of his operas," Greg said. Listeners would also erupt into spontaneous applause if they liked a particular moment in the music.

Greg grew up in Lake Elmo, Minnesota. Neither of his parents was a musician, but they considered music part of raising well-rounded kids. At the age of eight he started piano lessons, and he soon became so focused on music that his teacher would write in his weekly lesson notebook: "go outside and play."

He learned the bulk of his repertoire by sight-reading. Most weeks he would ride his bike to the local library and check out big stacks of sheet music – Chopin, Mozart, Tchaikovsky, and whatever else he could find. "My teacher didn't really know I was doing this. My parents didn't either. While they were in the house I would practice the repertoire I'd been assigned. Then I'd sight-read when they left." Grabbing random scores from the library worked out better some times than others. Once, after he'd only been playing a few years, he came home with the score for Tchaikovsky's "First Piano Concerto." "Oh wow," he thought when he saw the mass of notes covering the page, "it's so ... black!"

Greg's parents supported his passion for the piano, but they lived in a house that made it difficult not to hear every note he played as he practiced. When he was ten they built doors for the piano room. Later, they tried hanging curtains over the doors. They tried quilts, foam insulation, and heavy blankets. They researched sound-proofing techniques. One weekend when he was fourteen his brothers brought mattresses and pillows up from the basement and barricaded the room to try and dampen the sound. "I never knew if it worked – I just kept playing. After nine at night I had to stop and I never liked to be stopped. So naturally my brothers would relish being able to ask me to stop. To be honest, this probably coaxed me into practicing even more."

During his junior year in high school Greg began traveling nationally to various competitions. His teacher usually traveled with him and provided last-minute musical advice and tips on how to conquer his nerves. While other contestants played, Greg and his teacher would sit in the audience and pass notes back and forth with critiques of the performances. At a competition during his senior year, he heard Liz play for the first time. Usually, he found a lot to criticize, but in the note he passed to his teacher that day he had only one objection: the color of her dress. (It was green.)

During his senior year he sent audition tapes to *From the Top*. "A number of my friends had been on the show, and they said it was really fun. I was a bit envious of them, so I sent in an audition tape." In the spring he got a call. "They said, 'You'll be on the show in four weeks. What would you like to play?' They weren't very enthusiastic about the initial piece I suggested because another pianist had recently performed it on the show. I suggested another piece, even though I had never looked at the score before. I worked very, very hard preparing my piece (to the annoyance of my family and friends), and when the show came around, I was terribly nervous. Thankfully everything went fairly well." He ended up learning the Ravel "Toccata" in just under a month. He loved meeting host Christopher O'Riley and enjoyed the ethos of the show. "Christopher O'Riley is a decidedly un-stuffy pianist; he's a generous, warm, and likable guy, and he does a terrific job of making serious classical music accessible to young (and old!) audiences," Greg said. Looking back, he sees an analogy between his own work and *From the Top*. "Liz and I try to do something similar with our performances. In fact, our performances aren't so different from a *From the Top* show: we talk about the music we are playing and give personal anecdotes that engage our listeners; we play a huge variety of music; and we throw in spicy surprises that our audiences don't expect."

In the spring of his senior year, Greg was accepted to study at the Juilliard School. Despite his success at competitions and acceptance to *From the Top* and Juilliard, his parents were very concerned about his long-term prospects if he pursued music. In an effort to dissuade him from a life in music, his dad showed him the music section of a Best Buy ad: there wasn't a single classical CD advertised. His mom asked him to make a deal: if he wasn't famous by twenty-one he'd do something else. "At the time it was so frustrating, but looking back I think it was good they were realistic. For one thing it meant I kept going to public school and working hard on all my academic classes, so my whole world wasn't just music."

Now that Greg supports himself as a musician, his parents don't worry as much about his chosen career. And as non-musicians themselves, they represent precisely the type of audience member Greg and Liz work hard to attract. Each Anderson & Roe event is a mixture of narration, musical performance, and audience involvement. "I can't even imagine not talking," Greg told me. "Even for an educated audience, I want to talk about things that will interest everyone."

At the 2008 TED Conference – an annual event that gathers leaders from multiple fields to share ideas – Greg and Liz gave a presentation called "Mozart Rediscovered." The goal was to "present Mozart in a way that helps people shed critical layers," said Greg. They performed one of their own compositions, "Ragtime alla Turca," a virtuosic showpiece that revels in what Greg calls "the hoedown spirit of the original 'Rondo alla Turca.'" To illustrate the different characters of minor and major key sections of the music, they became Lachrymose Liz and Gregarious Greg, and literally embodied the music through their stage personas. They also talked about how performances of the piece have become increasingly tame and genteel, and explained that Mozart would have expected pianists to use Janissary pedals while playing to capture the Turkish flavor of the piece. (These pedals no longer exist on modern pianos, but were basically noise-making devices that produced drum, rattle, and bell and whistle sounds).

As part of his DMA at Yale, Greg is writing a book on the history of piano recital programming. Though the topic might seem arcane and dull, Greg hopes the book can use history to help answer a question fundamental to the survival of classical music: "What can we do as performers and programmers to make recitals more interesting?" The book is a natural extension of the work the duo already does in nearly every aspect of their public presentations, from their selection of repertoire, their music videos, and the design of their website (like everything they do, the website is interactive and personal, with photos, forums, blog posts, and question-and-answer sections). They've already put many ideas from the book into practice, and researching the history of performance is a way to expand their sense of what's possible while gaining a better understanding of how certain conventions became established. "It's a complicated subject, so some of this is oversimplifying, but in the twentieth century classical music has become over-intellectualized. It's often used more as a status symbol than a source of enjoyment. Part of this is because of the cults of greatness we've built around certain composers. We treat Schubert like a god, so we only play his greatest works. But we lose certain sides of his personality by promoting his cult of greatness. I think we need more balance in programming. We shouldn't just present the same pinnacles of Western music over and over again. Our musical culture tends to have this abhorrence of cheesiness – people are afraid of being vulnerable to direct emotion. If I listen to Schoenberg, and pretend to really love it, I get this strange intellectual power over my neighbor. I just want to cut through the posturing and lack of authenticity in the music world. But it's hard to write about this in a way that convinces intellectuals."

Though Greg devotes some of his time to constructing an intellectual case for the legitimacy of enjoying music, he spends even more energy putting theory into practice. Greg and Liz's desire to genuinely entertain and engage audiences isn't just a gambit. Many young artists are photographed in the most provocative and daring ways imaginable, but their concerts are utterly conventional. Greg and Liz's provocative photos aren't just marketing ploys, they're logical expressions of a particular vision of classical music. They don't want to lure audiences in with sexy photos and videos only to get down to business and perform a solemn, stolid recital of canonical masterpieces. Instead, they hook listeners by putting into practice an expanded concept of what classical music can be: sexy, funny, personal, and interactive.

To see part of their marketing strategy in action, I met them on the Upper West Side of Manhattan one afternoon for a guerrilla-style photo shoot to get new pictures for their website. A guerrilla photo shoot, as I soon learned, consists of sneaking into a semi-public place and using it as the backdrop for photos. We walked into a hostel on 102nd and Amsterdam Avenue with $3,500 of equipment in a briefcase. Avoiding eye contact with the desk clerk, we slipped up to the third floor and rapidly began setting up tripods, flash bulbs, and cameras. Their photographer had used the area before and thought the particular chocolate-colored hallway would provide a perfect back-drop for photos. In a matter of minutes, black extension cords were snaking along the hallway, two tripods with flash bulbs were adjusted to the proper heights, and Greg and Liz were giggling while striking dramatic poses against the walls. Greg wore a charcoal skinny suit with a metallic sheen, Liz wore a retro-gray sheath dress with a black belt worn high across her stomach and high heels. As the photographer snapped photos, their faces emerged briefly framed in pools of light splashed against the brown walls. Part of the excitement of the shoot came from the distinct possibility that at any moment we could be kicked off the premises.

None of the guests emerged from their rooms to find the hallway temporarily transformed into a photo shoot. But when they went to the next planned location, a tiled hallway off Mulberry Street in Chinatown, they attracted a crowd of puzzled on-lookers who watched the proceedings from doors and windows. At one point, some people told them to go away and then began shouting in Chinese. They were also unable to find an electric outlet until the photographer paid a Chinese man $20 to use the outlet in his kitchen. But the photos turned out great and the whole afternoon was, to use one of Greg's favorite phrases, "very Anderson and Roe."

The more time I spent with Greg and Liz, the more I began to see that everything they do is "very Anderson and Roe." Even for a small concert at a New Jersey Steinway dealership full of ersatz columns and gaudy chandeliers, Greg and Liz made every effort to engage the audience. There were roughly thirty people settled in small rows of metal folding chairs. "Looks like every pianist in New Jersey is here," Greg joked as they walked in.

Rather than making the typical virtuoso's stage entrance – sweeping on stage to a burst of applause and studiously avoiding eye contact with the audience – they began the concert by introducing themselves and saying a few words about piano teachers. "We wouldn't be here without people like you," Liz said. "I've had amazing teachers throughout my life," Greg added. "I still talk to my old piano teacher once a week." Soon Greg transitioned into his characteristic mode of address – a mixture of humor and instruction. "Now, duo piano is one of the few types of chamber music in which you are touching each other, which come to think of it, could put Brahms and Clara Schumann's relationship in a whole new light." He raised his eyebrows suggestively.

Throughout the recital, they prefaced each piece they played with either a personal comment – "To us this sounds almost like Mozart doing a musical rendering of laughter. So feel free to laugh at or with us" – or a bit of educational information – "This is the point in Bach's *St. Matthew Passion* when Peter realizes he has betrayed Christ, and the texture and dissonances evoke his weeping." Their comments throughout the recital performed the triple tasks of relaxing the audience, educating them and expanding their sense of what a classical recital can be. Near the end of their performance, during a rousing paraphrase of a Strauss waltz, a few pigtailed toddlers began dancing in the aisles. By the end of the waltz, it almost looked like some of the middle-aged New Jersey piano teachers might join them.

photo credit: Scott Gordon Bleicher

*Nine-year-old Greg dressed as a Sonatina for Halloween*

*At fourteen, practicing at home on his family's upright piano*

*Greg and Liz after one of their very first Anderson & Roe concerts*

*Anderson & Roe in perfomance*

# SECTION 2

## Meet the Competition

photo credit: Reid Mangan

# A Night at the Opera

The sheer number of classical musicians in the world – one estimate reports eighty million children in China alone are currently studying classical music – gives competitions a certain practical value in identifying major talent. While judges aren't infallible, they sometimes discover gifted musicians and give them deserved exposure. Fairly or not, winning a major competition has launched the career of many famous musicians. I wanted to see for myself what one of the world's most famous competitions is really like. That's how I met twenty-year-old soprano Nadine Sierra.

Five days before she was scheduled to compete in the national finals of the Metropolitan Opera National Council Auditions, Nadine woke earlier than usual with a scratchy throat and mild congestion. A cold is the singer's constant nightmare; the merest hint of symptoms usually provokes a frantic flurry of every kind of self-treatment imaginable.

A cold the week of the finals for the competition of the world's most famous opera house is a particularly cruel nightmare, especially if you've been dreaming of singing in the Met all your life.

Often dubbed the Met Contest by singers, the competition is considered the "American Idol" of the opera world. And while it is not yet televised, the Met Contest offers its share of drama, divas, potential stardom, and stinging commentary (though this is overheard in the aisles rather than publicly proclaimed by the judges).

Nadine has been in love with singing since she was a young girl. When she was five, her kindergarten teacher in Fort Lauderdale, Florida noticed that someone in the class was always singing the alphabet song, even when the rest of the students were quiet. At first, the teacher couldn't tell who it was. As soon as she tried to identify the source, the sound stopped. Eventually, she traced the singing to Nadine, who acquired the nickname "the ABC girl" from her peers. "I've always loved something that no one else did," she told me when we met for coffee on Manhattan's Upper West Side. Her parents were quick to notice her love of singing and at age six she started voice lessons. By the time she was eleven she knew opera was going to be her life.

In sixth grade, her class took a trip to New York City. They hit the usual tourist spots – Times Square, Central Park, the museums – but they also got tickets to see Rossini's comic opera *The Barber of Seville*. By the end of the opera, every other kid in the class was sound asleep. But Nadine was not only awake, she was transfixed. The grandeur of the stage and sets, the humor and drama of the story, and the beauty of the music held her spellbound. She returned to Florida knowing she wanted to be an opera singer.

Of course most kids want to be all sorts of things; trying on a profession is a bit like playing dress-up, you enjoy the costume for a while and then try on a different one. But Nadine's focus on opera was persistent. Her younger sister Melanie (also a singer) recalls, "I'd want to play Barbies with her and she'd be like 'no, I have to practice.'" Unlike Charles Yang, Nadine didn't need to be forced or bribed into practicing. She loved to sing. Standing just higher than the keys of the family's upright piano, she sang scales, exercises, and simple songs for an hour every day.

Her parents, a firefighter and a bank teller, were surprised by her interest, especially since neither of them is a musician. But her vocal talent was not without precedent. Her grandmother also liked to sing. "I knew Nadine had a special talent for singing – I had heard that same bell quality when my own mother sang," Nadine's mom told me. They encouraged her however they could. Her mom drove her to voice lessons and sat through every one to try and understand how she could best help Nadine practice at home. Nadine and Melanie watched movies of old musicals countless times and often reenacted their favorite scenes and songs while splashing about together in the family's backyard swimming pool. "She sang and swam almost nonstop. She spent *days* in our pool singing and swimming, pretending she was the little mermaid," her dad said.

By the time she was in high school, it was clear Nadine had a major and unusual talent for singing. After hearing a thirteen-year-old Nadine sing an aria, a famous soprano remarked, "I didn't have this voice until I was eighteen." A few months later she was invited to join the chorus of the Palm Beach Opera and soon joined the opera's young artist program. The other singers were in their mid-to-late-twenties. Nadine was fourteen.

The following year her piano teacher told her to audition for *From the Top*. She was accepted to appear on a live broadcast, so she and her mom drove to Atlanta, Georgia for the taping of the show. She sang Puccini's famous aria "O Mio Babbino Caro" from the opera *Gianni Schicchi*. The show was a wonderful experience – Chris played "sooo beautifully" – and she was thrilled to hear the show on the radio a few weeks later. (After hearing Nadine on the show, her sister Melanie was inspired to try voice lessons also. She's already been featured on *From the Top* twice).

Even by the standards of a typical over-stressed and over-achieving teen, Nadine's high school years were busy. She was up at 6 A.M. to catch the train to school; after school she had voice coaching, dinner, then rehearsal at the Palm Beach opera until 10 P.M., at which point she started her homework. With Nadine and Melanie both singing, it was a challenge for her parents to coordinate rides to rehearsals and lessons without interfering with their work schedules. "Had I worked full-time," her mom told me, "the kids wouldn't be where they are now." All the activities also took a toll on family time: "We were always going in different directions, the family was always split up. It wasn't the normal home where everyone goes home and has dinner together," her dad said.

By senior year in high school, Nadine began working with soprano Ruth Falcon, who teaches at the Mannes School of Music in New York. Ruth has taught many of the world's most famous sopranos. She also had a long career herself, performing throughout Europe and at the Metropolitan Opera in New York many times. Nadine's teacher in Florida, Khomal Khan, was a friend of Falcon's and the two coordinated their efforts. "It was like I was taking from

Ruth through Khomal," Nadine said. Though she was accepted by the Juilliard School and offered a full scholarship, Nadine chose to attend Mannes and continue with Ruth, choosing a teacher she trusted rather than a big-name conservatory. "The first lesson with Ruth was absolute ecstasy. I felt total ease, and that's exactly what she encourages; singing with ease, nothing pushed or strained," she said.

I first heard Nadine sing at a lesson with Ruth a few days before the national semi-finals of the Metropolitan Opera competition. Ruth teaches at a studio on Seventh Avenue a few blocks from Carnegie Hall. It was a warm day, but Nadine was drinking hot tea with lemon and honey, a magical elixir drunk by singers who want to prevent a cold, cure a cold, or simply relax their vocal cords. Nadine did not yet feel sick; she just wanted to relax her voice.

Hearing a singer in a large opera house is a very different experience than hearing one in a small studio. It's a bit like the difference between watching a seven-foot basketball player from the stands and standing next to one on the court. The sheer improbability of an immense physical gift becomes especially clear in close quarters. As Nadine started singing, I felt something in my skull reverberate at the frequency of her vibrato.

She began the lesson by singing strings of nonsense syllables, "yoyayoyayo" or "zeeaaheeoahee," which lets a singer exercise the different throat and facial muscles that naturally accompany different syllables. Even on her warm-ups, Nadine sang with an irrepressible musicality, like an actor who can't resist giving a Shakespearian flourish even when reciting the contents of a grocery list. The seemingly mundane musical exercises blossomed into small feats of expressiveness, miniature arias with artfully shaped phrases and graceful hand gestures.

One of Ruth's colleagues was visiting from Australia and sat in on the lesson. Noticing her stunned expression when she heard Nadine's voice, Ruth nodded proudly and said, "Her voice is like cream, like thick juicy cream." The woman, still in a state of shock, murmured, "It's unbelievable."

For the Met Competition, Nadine prepared four opera arias in three different languages. Though the judges generally hear only two arias, they might request any of the four. Nadine's repertoire for the competition consisted of arias by Mozart (German), Gounod (French), Mascagni (Italian), and Moore (English). At Mannes, she studies the diction and pronunciation of the major European languages essential for opera: French, German, and Italian. Using a dictionary, she always translates the arias she sings into English and reads a libretto or summary to understand the dramatic context of the aria in the opera. The plots of many famous operas are notoriously hard to take seriously, but even the most outlandish situation or improbable emotion can gain true urgency if the music and performer are sufficiently persuasive. Nadine naturally modulates her body language and facial expressions to imbue the stock operatic predicaments of love and betrayal, loyalty and vengeance, with a palpable reality.

As Nadine sang through the repertoire for the competition, first the Australian woman and then even Ruth, began dabbing their eyes.

Ruth's suggestions were fairly minimal; now and then she encouraged Nadine to sing a certain note louder, or to build more toward a climax in a given passage. But this close to the competition, the essentials of diction, dynamics, and phrasing were secure.

When she finished, Nadine heard Ruth's opinions on various New York agents, many of whom were already interested in representing her. Having seen other young singers launch into a demanding professional career at a young age and suffer both vocally and personally, Ruth was anxious that Nadine avoid a similar fate. Her protectiveness was understandable. Nadine is the youngest student Ruth has ever taught who has made it so far in the Met Competition. If she won, the pressure to begin a career would be stronger than ever. But the life of an opera singer can damage the vocal cords of a young singer whose voice is still developing. Major opera roles require enormous physical exertion that taxes even experienced professionals. For a younger voice, the strain can cause permanent damage.

Advancing to the semi-finals was already a major achievement. After advancing through preliminary stages, Nadine was one of the five chosen from thirty-five contestants in her district. Then, at the regional competition in Boston, she was the only one of sixteen singers picked to advance to the national semi-finals. By the time she got to New York, more than fifteen hundred singers from fifteen regions across the country had been winnowed down to a select group of twenty-three national semi-finalists.

Two days before the semi-finals, Nadine met the other singers at an orientation on the Metropolitan Opera stage. The upper age limit for the competition is thirty, and most of the contestants were in their late twenties. At twenty, Nadine was much younger than everyone else in the room. The director of the competition introduced herself and congratulated the singers, emphasizing that they were now in a different league; they were on the verge of major careers and management contracts. She reminded them that the invitees to the semi-finals on Sunday were powerful people in the opera world – agents, managers, and artistic programmers. In short, they were potential employers. A good performance could be the start of a major career.

After the orientation, the semi-finalists got a special tour of the Met's labyrinthine backstage passages and chambers. It was Nadine's first time backstage, and more than anything else she was overwhelmed by the sheer size of things. There were hundreds of employees, seven floors, dozens of dressing rooms and rehearsal spaces, and so many sets for several different operas. "Everything is big – the name, the stage, the reputations of the singers, the salaries," she said.

After the tour, Nadine had a quick lesson with Ruth and sang lightly – only parts of arias and not at full volume – in order to save her voice for Sunday. Then she returned to the Met for a pizza dinner and a performance of the opera *Adriana Lecouvreur* with the tenor Placido Domingo singing the lead.

❦ ❦ ❦

The day before the semi-finals Nadine relaxed, slept, and cooked a Valentine's Day dinner of pasta with mushroom sauce and toasted baguettes with her roommates, both of whom are also singers studying at Mannes.

Singers were asked to arrive at the Met by 11 A.M. on Sunday, but Nadine was awake by 7:30, preparing her usual concoction of hot tea, lemon, and honey. The next few hours were devoted to hair and make-up, which can play a decisive role in competitions. The ideal outfit, according to Nadine, is a compromise between extremes. If a gown is too strikingly glamorous, it can overshadow the singer. On the other hand, if a gown is conspicuously plain, you risk not making a memorable impression. A gown should be tight enough to accentuate one's figure, but not so tight that it interferes with breathing.

With the Met's new emphasis on live HD broadcasts of opera to movie theaters around the world, the appearance and sensuality of singers has become more important than ever. The classic opera joke of a three-hundred-pound soprano playing a seductive heroine who drives men mad with lust has become an increasingly rare reality in today's opera houses, where most casting directors favor slender singers provocatively (un)dressed. While some claim the obsession with attractive singers comes at the expense of musical quality, a generation of new stars is proving that a dramatically plausible appearance is compatible with wonderful singing.

The child of a Portuguese mother and a Puerto Rican father, Nadine has coffee-colored skin, dark eyes, and a slightly exotic, Mediterranean appearance. Her tall, striking figure could easily meet the new visual standards of the opera world. In fact, her first year in New York, she was accosted by a man who told her bluntly, "you should be a model."

For the semi-finals she wore a flowing cream-colored gown that nicely offset her skin color. Nadine uses the meticulousness of her physical grooming to compensate for the volatility and uncertainty of live performance. She's a perfectionist ("total control-freak") in her visual preparation, but once onstage, she relinquishes control, trusts her training and hopes for the best.

Some fortunate combination of age and temperament enables Nadine to transform nervousness into excitement. While other singers waiting backstage pace frantically, clench their hands, and generally freak out, Nadine finds a nice patch of carpeted floor, kicks off her three-inch heels, and lies down. She stretches, does yoga, and hums along with the aria another contestant is rehearsing. But she retains a certain peacefulness that not only makes her life easier, it makes her singing better. Nerves mean tension, and tension affects breath control and tone quality, two essentials for a good vocal performance.

By 11 A.M., Nadine was settled backstage in a dressing room she shared with another soprano. It was a large room with mirrored walls, dozens of light bulbs framing the mirrors, an upright piano, and a couch. Given the Met's long and star-studded history, she couldn't help but wonder who had sat in this room before, fixing a stray hair before a debut, collapsing in a glow of sweat and make-up after a triumphant aria.

By a quarter to noon, roughly one hundred people had arrived and taken seats in the grand tier level. These were the friends, family and teachers of the twenty-three contestants as well as talent scouts, managers, and other influential people in the opera world. On the lowest level of the opera house, the orchestra floor, seven judges sat scattered across a few rows, close enough to confer but markedly separate from everyone else. The stage was bare except for a grand piano in the center and a crescent of wood panels curved behind the piano to bounce the sound out into the house. With the vast majority of seats empty, and the chandeliers glistening on plush red seats and aisles, the opera house seemed ominously large and majestic, like a huge deserted mansion.

No more than ten of the twenty-three semi-finalists advance to the finals. Each sings two arias – the first of their choosing, the second requested by the judges from among their prepared repertoire. Nadine sang seventh of the twenty-three singers. Just after 1 P.M. she heard the announcement, "Ms. Sierra, stage right, Ms. Sierra, stage right," in her dressing room. She reminded herself that professional opera singers did this all the time. In fact, they did more than this. If they could sing a three-hour opera to thousands of fans, she could sing for ten minutes to a few hundred people.

From the stage, the opera house appeared smaller than she expected and the dazzling lights above made her feel as if she were looking up to the heavens. She began with an aria called "Ruhe Sanft, Mein Holdes Leben" from an early Mozart opera, *Zaide*. The aria is a tender love song – the title means "rest gently, my sweet love." It's a good luck aria for Nadine, one she's sung hundreds of times and knows perfectly. More than speed or agility, it showcases tone and musicality, two of her great strengths.

After finishing the first aria, a microphoned voice from the audience requested the aria known as "Juliette's Waltz" from the nineteenth century French composer Charles Gounod's operatic take on *Romeo and Juliet*. The opening lyrics could be translated as "I want to live/In this dream which intoxicates me/This day still,/sweet flame/I keep you in my soul." It's a flirtatious and fast aria that demands a good deal of vocal agility, something Nadine has worked diligently to develop. As her voice raced up and down scales, she swayed coyly, gestured languorously, and let the musical pulse carry her a small distance across the stage. Everything about her presence enhanced the young-girl-in-love quality of the words and music. As soon as the last note sounded, the audience burst into the loudest applause yet of the afternoon. As she walked off-stage, the stage manager gave her a one-word assessment: "Damn." In the audience, I caught excited snippets of whispering – "She's only twenty." "Did you know she got into Juilliard at seventeen?"

Back in the dressing room, Nadine lay down on the couch and tried to sleep to pass the time. But she was too excited to nap, her limbs felt jittery and her blood was pounding. Ruth texted her: "Fabulous, biggest applause, everyone wants to hear you sing more." She knew that in one sense, she had already won – she'd worked hard and sung her best. Still, the stakes were higher than any competition she'd been in before.

While Nadine went out for Chinese with a few friends, I stayed to listen to the rest of the contestants. Of the first seven, she had been a clear standout, but as the afternoon dragged on I began to realize how many subjective factors could sway one's evaluation of a performance. First, there was a singer's appearance – their dress, gender, age, attractiveness, height, weight, etc. Next, there were their dramatic movements; some singers were fairly restrained, while others were totally in character. One tenor, singing a Verdi aria about seduction, rakishly loosened his tie and ogled the audience. Finally, there was one's taste in opera: if a singer happened to choose one of the judges' favorite arias, they might confuse their love of the piece with the quality of the performance, or they might judge even the slightest mistake more harshly on an aria they loved. From the interaction of all these subjective forces, a decision that aspired to objectivity would somehow arise. I started to see why so many musicians considered competitions hopelessly unfair.

When the final singer finished, it was nearly 5 P.M. The judges conferred for almost half an hour while the friends, family, and musical elite made increasingly anxious small talk on the tier level. The last of the afternoon's weak February light fell through the opera house's glass façade. Finally, a woman emerged, and the twenty-three singers appeared and clustered in anxious groups behind her. She took a sheet of paper from her pocket and got right to the point. "The 2009 finalists are…" Each singer stepped forward as their name was announced to a burst of applause. As she read each name, I checked the judges' choices against the preferences I'd jotted down while listening. I had marked each of the twenty-three singers with a yes, maybe, or no. Several of my 'maybes' were chosen to advance to the finals, and several of my 'yeses' were not (none of my 'nos' advanced). She read seven names. Nadine was not among them.

At the last possible moment, she said "Nadine Sierra." Nadine broke into a huge smile, stepped forward and hugged the other finalists. She was a singer the judges and I both agreed was a yes.

♩ ♩ ♩

Two days later, just five days before the finals, Nadine woke up with the first symptoms of a cold. She tried everything she could to get better, which mostly meant staggering amounts of tea, sleep and vitamin C. Even if her voice croaked like a toad, she wasn't going to miss the chance to perform at the Met.

The week before the competition was crammed with activities: there were breathing technique sessions, dramatic movement coaching sessions, rehearsals with piano, rehearsals with orchestra, photographers from the *New York Times*, and a meeting with Met board members. The eight finalists were also offered tickets to all the operas at the Met that week, but Nadine skipped them to get as much rest as possible.

The cold felt a bit better on Wednesday, but when she hadn't shaken it by Thursday she became scared. She had dire visions of bronchitis, laryngitis, months of bed-rest. Despite her attempts to sleep, she was getting only about six hours a night. Her habitual calm was finally ruffled; she woke up singing parts of her arias in her head, thinking about things to change, German words to pronounce, musical phrases to accentuate and shape. She also dreamed she walked on stage the day of the finals, opened her mouth and forgot everything.

But the activities at the Met were going well. She was getting to know and like the other finalists, she was learning from a variety of experts, and she was being praised by many accomplished singers and musicians. An influential Met staff member asked her the not-so-subtle question, "What are your plans after college?" Given who was asking the question, Nadine understood the remark was a fairly strong hint she would be able to find a place in the Met's coveted young artist program.

On Friday, she still felt sick, but not "sick sick"– an all-important distinction. She rehearsed with the orchestra at the Met, had a meet-and-greet with the competition's national network of judges and board members, and later in the day met her parents and her sister Melanie at their hotel just across the street from Lincoln Center and the Metropolitan Opera House. Her family had flown in from Florida that morning and seemed even more nervous than Nadine.

On Saturday, the day before the finals, she bought a humidifier and got a massage. She spent the bulk of the day with her parents, with just a short coaching with Ruth in the late afternoon. But her voice didn't feel right; it wasn't responding the way it usually did. When she returned to her apartment, she found her bedroom transformed. Her sister and roommates had placed smoothies loaded with extra vitamin C around the room, incense and lighted candles on the dressers and tables, and plugged the humidifier in next to her bed.

She went straight to bed, but slept horribly. She had the same nightmare about forgetting everything and woke repeatedly, worrying about the cold, worrying about the worries that kept her from the sleep that could cure the cold…

Somehow the night passed and suddenly it was the morning she had been waiting for. She made her customary thermos of hot tea, lemon, and honey, took a long hot shower, and called her mom, who told her everything would be okay.

The finals were at 3 P.M. By 10 A.M., she was at Ruth's apartment for a quick warm-up. Ruth thought she sounded much better than the day before ("You sounded like shit yesterday … But today you sound great") and through some combination of vitamin C, adrenaline, and humid air, Nadine felt better, too.

By 11 A.M. she was at the Met. This time she had an entire dressing room to herself. After running through snippets of her arias onstage, she settled into the soothing task of doing her hair and makeup. She also continued drinking a steady stream of tea drowned in honey and fruit juice. At 2 P.M. she joined the other finalists for a photo shoot onstage and by 2:15 huge crowds were forming in the lobby of the Met, the usual scalpers cruising the throngs with spare tickets.

Unlike the closed semifinals, the finals were open to the opera-loving public. Instead of singing for one hundred people, she would perform for close to four thousand. But among the masses would be her family and nearly fifty friends and classmates from the Mannes School of Music.

There were eight national finalists who would compete that afternoon, four men and four women. Each would sing two arias, one on the first half of the program and one on the second. A guest artist, the soprano Dolora Zajick, would perform briefly at the end of the concert to give the judges time to deliberate. Then up to five winners would be announced from the stage. Each winner would receive a prize of $15,000 and capture the attention of the most important people in the opera world.

About an hour before the competition began, Nadine's dad tried to make his way backstage to see her. Even though he has been watching her perform for more than a decade, he still becomes "a nervous wreck" when she performs. He said that today, "felt like the Superbowl, and I'm playing in it." But he was also confident – five winners out of eight finalists are decent odds, and he thinks Nadine is capable of anything. Unable to get backstage, he waited in the lobby, pacing through the crowd and trying to stay calm.

In her dressing room before the performance, Nadine felt her usual calm. As she would put it, she stayed "chillaxed." But the friends she had made during the week seemed once again like competitors, each focused on their arias and disinclined to make small talk. Not even Nadine is immune to the latent hostility that runs beneath the surface of most major competitions. However friendly they were, the other singers were ultimately competitors vying for a very small number of spots.

The finals were hosted by baritone Thomas Hampson, a past winner of the event. In his introductory remarks, he told the audience that over one hundred current Met artists have come through the competition: if not a prerequisite for stardom, it certainly made it more likely.

Once again, Nadine would perform seventh on the program, but this time she would begin with "Juliette's Waltz." While the first six singers performed, Nadine did floor stretches, massaged her facial muscles, and even sang along with the arias she had come to know over the past week. Finally, she heard the loudspeaker: "Nadine Sierra, stage right."

As she walked onstage she noticed she could only see the first six rows of the audience, but could feel a tremendous energy and tension in the air. I felt my stomach tighten as she walked out. I'd enjoyed the first six performances, but watching someone you know perform at a major competition is always stressful – an aria morphs from an aesthetic pleasure into a dangerous musical minefield. Every difficult passage or high note is a potential disaster. If I was clutching the arms of my chair, I could only imagine how her parents were feeling. But Nadine imbued the aria with the same breathless, love-struck quality as the week before, nailed all the tricky fast sections and high notes, and flung her arms open as if to embrace the audience on the final note. The audience exploded with applause and shouts that began even before the orchestra had played the last note. As she walked off stage she smiled – she knew she'd done well. Backstage in her dressing room, her phone was jammed with text messages from friends, family, and Ruth. If this were the Superbowl, as her dad said, she'd just scored a touchdown.

In the second half, Nadine's Mozart aria was basically an out-of-body experience. She had no memory of what happened while she was onstage, only hearing the waves of applause that began before she finished. This time there were no ecstatic texts from friends; they were waiting to hear the results.

For those not interested in opera, the competition holds a secondary fascination as a fashion show. There were no surprises with the four male singers – all wore the standard suit or tuxedo. But each of the four females wore a sumptuous gown; one was scarlet encrusted with red rhinestones, one was royal purple. Nadine wore a blue gown with minimal frills that exposed her shoulders. Her hair, like the gold curtains of the Met's stage, was upswept and pinned in ornate folds.

The guest artist sang an aria from Verdi's *Macbeth*, and Nadine and the other contestants clustered in the wings of the stage to listen. Everyone seemed relieved to be finished. Both the performance by the guest artist and the long-winded comments by Thomas Hampson that followed were calculated to give the judges as much time as possible to deliberate. There was no argument or filibustering by any of the judges. Each judge simply ranked the singers from one to eight. The scores of all the judges were added together, and the four singers with the lowest totals were the winners.

Finally, someone interrupted Hampson and handed him a piece of paper. He read the first name. It wasn't Nadine. He read the second name. It wasn't Nadine. He read the third name. Not Nadine. The first three winners assembled onstage, each shaking Hampson's hand after his name was announced. Then he said, "We do have one more winner this year, she's our only female winner." Nadine's chances had dropped from five in eight to one in four. Her mom was worried: "When they called the three guys and said there was one female winner, my heart was beating faster than ever. You just never know, especially having someone so young competing." As in the semifinals, I'd been keeping track of my own picks for the afternoon and some of my winners weren't chosen while some of my maybes were proclaimed winners. Nadine was also anxious; she'd sung well but there were so many factors she couldn't control. Before there was more time to worry, Hampson cleared his throat and shouted:

"NADINE SIERRA!"

She walked out across the stage beaming. She was listening to the loudest ovation of her life. Her friends were screaming and cheering and her family and Ruth were crying ecstatic tears.

Watching the champagne reception following the event, it struck me how easily things could have turned out differently. If her cold had been a bit more stubborn, her nerves a bit less steady, or the judges prejudiced by her young age, she could easily have been comforted rather than congratulated at the reception. But at least in the case of one young musician in one competition, everything worked the way it's supposed to and a truly unusual talent was recognized and celebrated. She'd receive a check for $15,000 and the attention of everyone in the opera world. She was one of the youngest singers ever to win the competition.

As Nadine flitted between groups of friends and sponsors under the light of huge chandeliers, I thought of her description of the character Juliette in Gounod's opera. "She's very young – and she's singing about being free and young and having desires she can't explain. She's a little crazy, but she's happy to be crazy and she's just enjoying being young and sweet." She could almost have been talking about herself.

*Nadine visiting the Met in sixth grade.*

*Nadine at fifteen performing on From the Top*

*Nadine with her parents, Robert and Melinda (above), and below with her teacher Ruth Falcon (far left) and a friend at the Metropolitan Opera competition*

photo credit: Chris Lee

# How to Win a Seat in the New York Philharmonic

The morning of his preliminary audition for a seat in the New York Philharmonic, trumpeter Matt Muckey caught the downtown train to Lincoln Center from Harlem, where he was staying with a friend. He arrived in midtown Manhattan extremely early. He carried his trumpet and a Sony Gameboy.

A twenty-one year-old senior at Northwestern's School of Music, Matt was one of the youngest musicians at the preliminaries.

The preliminaries weren't actually preliminary. Everyone at the audition had already cleared an initial screening and been invited to compete. Musicians are typically selected on the strength of a resume, and a few other orchestras had denied Matt a chance to audition because of his age. But the New York Philharmonic accepted a broader range of applicants.

The New York Philharmonic wasn't his first orchestra audition, but it was certainly the most prestigious. Many musicians consider auditions an art distinct from music-making. "It's a game," Matt told me later, "and like any game you can improve by learning the specific rules it follows and playing it multiple times."

He'd already played the game in San Francisco as a college junior, and in his senior year he was auditioning in Los Angeles, Chicago, and many smaller orchestras around the country. Though Matt learned from the various auditions he had taken before the New York Philharmonic, they weren't all positive experiences. During a semi-final in Oregon, while playing a particularly high and loud excerpt from Strauss' *Also Sprach Zarathustra*, he passed out and fell off his chair. "I'd forgotten to take a breath, and as I was holding the last note I started going black, then I fell off the chair, luckily onto a padded floor, and I came to shortly after.

"It's trauma, taking an audition. It's not a relaxing experience at all. You get dry mouth, you're short of breath, maybe your fingers are shaking. One of the most disappointing feelings is to go into an audition, have your playing evaluated, and be told it's not good enough. You've invested months of practice, money for the flight and hotel, you've fronted all of this and now you're expected to play like you're relaxed?"

One of the most challenging aspects of auditioning for a major orchestra is maintaining a calm and focused state to promote an optimal performance. For a trumpeter this challenge is particularly acute: somatic manifestations of nervousness such as rapid breathing and heart rate or clenched stomach muscles interfere directly with the breath control necessary to produce a good tone and accurate pitch.

Following the standard convention for most auditions, Matt and the other trumpeters waited in a common room at Lincoln Center. In other words, they sat facing their competition. "You try not to look at them," Matt said, articulating what seems to be a general policy among auditioners. "People usually stay quiet and politely ignore each other." According to one common piece of audition lore, this etiquette has such force that when a student once encountered a former teacher auditioning for the same job, neither greeted or acknowledged the other.

As Matt settled into his seat, he recognized many faces from previous auditions. A fairly stable group of regulars tend to cycle through the audition circuit, a pattern that reflects the reality that there are far more musicians than jobs.

Many people buried themselves in books or listened to iPods; Matt played world cup soccer and Nascar racing on his Gameboy.

When he was finally called to play, he had an unpleasant surprise: he would have to walk up two flights of stairs to get to the audition hall. "It seems minor, but if I'd panicked it could have been bad. Having to walk up stairs carrying a fifteen-pound trumpet case meant I'd be just slightly winded, and without perfect breath control it's harder to play at your best."

The seat for which Matt was auditioning had been open for years. Despite a national search, no one had played well enough to meet the standards of the search committee. In other words, even playing better than everyone else would be no guarantee of winning the spot. He would have to meet an absolute standard of quality.

Part of what makes auditions so daunting is not knowing what you'll be asked to play. Rather than simply preparing and performing a fixed repertoire, musicians are given a dizzying number of possible orchestral works and told that excerpts from any are fair game. The process is similar to the comprehensive exams many doctoral students take: they're given a list of hundreds of books and can be quizzed and questioned on anything covered in any one of them. Of course, there are ways for musicians to predict which excerpts are most likely to be requested. Difficult passages tend to be picked more often than easy ones, and the most common works of the orchestral repertoire tend to be picked more than relatively obscure ones.

When he caught his breath after climbing the stairs, Matt walked across a strip of carpet shielded behind a large opaque screen. The carpeting was designed to muffle the sound of heels clicking across the floor. This measure was meant to ensure that the committee of orchestral musicians judging the audition would not be biased, even subconsciously, by the gender of the musician. The screen behind which Matt played served a similar function, blocking out extraneous and potentially biasing features like age and appearance.

"I felt comfortable knowing that I wasn't stigmatized for being young," Matt said. "It was just about how you play. But of course I had high anxiety. You're playing in their hall, for their best players. These are people you've looked up to your whole life and now you're playing for the chance to join them." Matt was asked to play excerpts from Strauss, Mussorgsky, Ravel, Mahler, and Respighi.

In some orchestral auditions, results are given immediately – picture the "thanks … next!" model of show business and musical theater. At the NY Phil preliminaries the musicians waited to hear if they would advance. "I did the best I could so I didn't stress over it as I waited." Around thirty minutes later he learned he'd advanced to the semi-finals. Two months later he would return for the next round. He flew back to Northwestern the next day.

♩ ♩ ♩

Matt didn't spend his childhood dreaming of a life in music. He began playing the trumpet when he was nine, and initially practiced only a half an hour each day.

In part, his short practice sessions reflected the physical demands of playing the trumpet. A trumpeter produces sound by controlling the combination of airflow and lip vibration: the former regulates volume while the latter, in conjunction with valves and pistons, determines pitch. Young children lack the lung capacity to make a decent sound on the instrument, and even adult players have to limit their practice time so their lips and facial muscles don't become overly fatigued.

But Matt's limited practice time also reflected his parents' desire to ensure that music was just one part of his childhood. "I played soccer, I played golf. I was a kid. I was totally interested in other things," he said.

His parents encouraged consistency and hard work in all his endeavors, so music was a small but constant presence. "We'd go to Florida on vacation and I'd have to bring my trumpet and practice. Looking back that sort of thing really shows me how much they cared and how much they valued hard work."

His mom had been a trumpet minor in college, so she often guided Matt's practice sessions. "It wasn't always easy at the time. My mom would sit down and say 'Play this, now play that, try it this way.' But not everyone has a parent like that. She guided me. She developed my general knowledge of music, my expression and dynamics."

Some of his best memories of playing come from standing on his back deck in rural California and listening to the sound of his trumpet echoing back across the valley. (The earliest record of the trumpet dates back to around 1500 B.C., and for most of the instrument's history it was used outdoors, often as a signaling device for armies.)

While Matt loved the powerful sound of a trumpet played outdoors, his neighbors did not. They once called his parents to complain that he was practicing outside at 6 A.M., before school. The sheer noise of his instrument also caused problems in other venues. Whenever his mom took him to play at nursing homes in the Sacramento area, the volume of his playing invariably raised a chorus of beeping and malfunctioning hearing aids to punctuate his performance.

Matt had a natural affinity for the instrument and learned the repertoire easily, but he measured himself against daunting examples. "I grew up listening to Wynton Marsalis, so that kept me humble." He also grew up listening to recordings by Phil Smith, principal trumpet for the New York Philharmonic. Years later, Smith would be on the selection committee that listened to Matt's audition.

In high school, he became more serious about music, but it still didn't seem like something to which he would devote his life. "Lots of people know they'll be musicians, I just enjoyed playing. In high school I thought maybe I'd be a doctor, a psychiatrist. I studied a lot, did AP classes, trumpet was just on the side."

With his youth orchestra he traveled through Switzerland, Austria, and Italy, where in Venice, he and two other trumpeters rented a gondola and played the Jean-Baptiste Arban arrangement of *Carnival of Venice*. "I think classical music definitely gives young people opportunities they wouldn't have otherwise, and traveling was one of those opportunities for me."

In the spring of his senior year, he appeared on a San Francisco taping of *From the Top*. "*From the Top* was an awesome experience, to say the least. There was an audience of 3,000 people. I'd never performed on that large a scale before. I was more scared than for anything I'd ever done before, but really excited." He played the *Carnival of Venice*, and the experience boosted his confidence. "It was one of the coolest things I've ever done. They give young musicians the chance to become soloists on a national stage; they're like a star-finder. Since I was young I always heard these kids on the show who were fantastic."

The spring of his senior year, he also heard back from college and conservatory auditions. He was wait-listed at Juilliard, accepted by Northwestern and offered a full ride to the University of Wyoming. "Getting into Northwestern, that's when I committed to music. I knew my parents would be investing money in it and I started getting more serious. You really need that sense of responsibility. In college, there are no parents to make sure you practice."

He was expecting to be one of the worst trumpeters in his studio at Northwestern, but after a few months on campus he didn't feel so hopelessly behind. "As a freshman I found out I could keep up with the other players and learn from them. One of Northwestern's great strengths is how the teachers encourage the students to learn from one another." He also enjoyed the intellectual focus of students out-side the music school. "Most of the people I hung out with in college are now doctors or in graduate school."

Matt's teacher at Northwestern, Charlie Geyer, had won a seat in the Chicago Symphony Orchestra at the age of twenty-two. So when Matt, as a sophomore, showed an interest in making audition tapes to try to get invited to various preliminary rounds, his teacher was supportive and familiar with the process of trying to master a huge range of excerpts. "Charlie had a library of scores, so I made a bootleg book with almost all the excerpts."

Geyer's approach didn't focus exclusively on mastering excerpts. Instead, they were just one part of a broader plan of preparation. "What people don't realize is that you don't need to just work on excerpts. You need to work on being a good trumpeter."

♪ ♪ ♪

Matt took his preliminary audition at the New York Philhar-monic in January, but the semifinals weren't until March. In the intervening months he developed a multifaceted training regimen designed to give him the best possible chance of advancing to the finals. Every day he played etudes for one to two hours to develop the lip muscle stamina needed if called on to play multiple rounds at the audition. He also began listening to music for hours each day. He and Charlie compiled a list of 300 works from which excerpts were most likely to be drawn and Matt tried to listen to every piece on the list. He'd sit in the music library with headphones, a pencil, and a full orchestral score of the works he was listening to. "Most people know thirty to forty seconds of a work insanely well, which in a way makes them blind. Orchestras know this so they ask for the less standard parts on excerpts."

Listening to repertoire in its entirety helped him internalize subtleties of phrasing and stylistic nuances appropriate to various periods and composers. To further hone his musicianship, he often asked other trumpeters to play duets so he could practice blending his tone and matching his interpretation with other players.

In addition to musical preparation he also tried to simulate the psychological challenges of a major audition. Geyer's advice was simple: try to make yourself nervous. "I'd write down the names of all the excerpts on scraps of paper and put them into a hat. Then I'd go find some random violist in the hallway and say, 'Hey, can you listen to me for a second?'"

As the semifinals approached, he began fitting miniature practice sessions into odd spare moments of the day. Several nights a week he worked as a driver for the campus escort service from 8 P.M. to 3 A.M. While waiting for a call to pick someone up, he'd practice in short bursts in the driver's seat. "My friends would tease me, they'd see me parked somewhere practicing and come bang on the windows and shout 'Dude, take us to McDonalds!'"

On nights when he wasn't working, he'd sneak into an old recital hall on campus. He'd slip into an open window and play on the darkened stage where generations of other musicians had performed and rehearsed. "I started to think the place was haunted. It's such an old building. I'd wander around while resting and hear these little noises, these rustlings and this constant whooshing of the pipes. Then as I walked home later I'd look back and there'd be one single light glowing in the attic."

On top of his audition preparation he was still a full-time university student, so he had to attend classes and keep up with assignments. To avoid burnout, he played video games during breaks in the day. "My parents said, 'Oh, those video games, they'll distract you.' And they did, that was the point."

The day before the semi-finals, Matt flew to New York. He stayed in New Jersey at a friend's house where he had an entire floor to himself to practice. If the atmosphere in the audition room at the preliminary round had been intense, the semi-finals were a whole new level. "Some people get super friendly, some are totally quiet – both are expressions of nerves."

Some of the musicians took beta-blockers and a variety of other pills to try to quell their anxiety. One musician joked that the people at any major audition have enough pills to stock a small pharmacy. "It was not a fun environment. Everyone there loves music, but this is a different thing. There's a switch from enjoyment to employment. I knew that I was prepared, but there's always doubt. Lots of people go to auditions their whole life and it's not their day. In ten to twenty minutes you're playing all the hardest things on your instrument and you have to do it perfectly."

At the second round Matt not only played excerpts, he was asked to play duets with Phil Smith, the orchestra's principal trumpet. The screen from the first round was still set up, but Smith came out from behind the screen to play. Since he saw Matt, he didn't vote in the round. "They want to hear your blend quality, how well you can match tone and pitch with another player. I'd grown up listening to him and I idolized him. To younger players, the brass section of the New York Philharmonic is untouchable. They're like gods among trumpet players. They wear tuxes every night, drive nice cars, and they're able to live in New York City by playing the trumpet."

After the audition he called his parents. "They asked how it went and I told them, 'I don't care – I got to play with Phil Smith.'" Later that day he found out he had advanced to the finals. He and two other trumpeters would compete at the end of the month. He was somewhat shocked by the news. "I never had the idea that I was this incredible player. If you asked me then I'd never, never, never have told you that I could win a seat in a top five orchestra."

He became obsessed with preparation after the semi-finals. For the final round the format changed: he would play a solo piece in addition to excerpts from orchestral repertoire. The screen from the first two rounds would also disappear: he would be visible as he played. He chose works by Haydn and Hummel and decided to play without sheet music. "It gives a gift to the audience to play without music. I wanted to move them, to try and communicate something with my playing. Technicality is extremely important; you have to know the notes, the style, the tempo of every excerpt. But ultimately, they care more about you doing something that inspires them than they do about perfection. You have to do something that makes them put down their pencils and enjoy your playing."

He continued and intensified his preparation regime of playing etudes, listening to entire works, performing for randomly chosen people, late-night practice sessions, and video games. The intensity of this schedule made keeping up with class work difficult. And he would have to miss even more classes to compete in the finals. A few days before he flew in for the finals, his conducting professor told him if he missed one more class he would fail him.

With only three trumpeters competing, his odds had improved dramatically. From an initial pool of more than five hundred trumpeters, he was now one of three. When he walked on stage at Lincoln Center's Avery Fisher Hall he could see Phil Smith, conductor Lorin Maazel, and other New York Philharmonic players and personnel sitting in the audience. He closed his eyes and began to play.

He got the results later that day. "Imagine your happiest moment in life; that was how I felt. I went from being a student to saying I'm in the New York Philharmonic. They asked me when could I start and I'd been accepted to this student festival in the summer, so without thinking I said I may not be able to make it this summer. Then I thought about what I'd just said, called them back and said 'I'll cancel that festival.'"

By the time he got back to campus the next day the news had already spread that he'd won the position. He found himself a minor celebrity on campus and a major one within the music school. The professor who threatened to fail him suddenly didn't seem so concerned about his attendance. When he gave his senior recital a few weeks later, in the same hall where he snuck in late at night to practice, the audience was overflowing. People had driven in from around the state to hear him. "I was almost as nervous for that as I had been for the audition. Everyone wanted to find out who's this kid who got into the New York Philharmonic?"

By the time he graduated, other music students had begun buying and playing handheld video game systems, hoping this might be the key to success.

♪ ♪ ♪

One April day in 2009, three years after he joined the New York Philharmonic, Matt walked into a small studio on the first floor of the Juilliard School. He was giving a master class to several trumpeters in Juilliard's Pre-College program. It was a satisfying and symbolic moment: he was coming back to teach at the institution that had wait-listed him seven years before. It also highlighted the element of luck in all auditions and competitions. He started the class by playing the slow movement of the Böhme trumpet concerto. Then he worked with each of the six students, listening to them play before offering tips on musicality, technique, and breath support.

After the class he had a few hours to relax before playing a concert that night. After three years in the orchestra, the shock of playing with former heroes as colleagues still hasn't disappeared. "Some nights I just sit there listening and I can't believe I'm actually in the New York Philharmonic. It just seems so improbable."

But while the job is ideal in many ways, it's also been challenging to adjust to the schedule and constant strain of life in a major orchestra. "The schedule doesn't allow for a normal life. We work when others rest and relax. By the time I get home from concerts I'm exhausted. It's not really that late, but the strain of concentrating so intensely for so long is very tiring."

In a certain sense, playing in the Philharmonic resembles a constant audition. Rather than competing against others, he's competing against his own nerves and anxiety. "My fear of mishaps hasn't become a reality, but the pressure at this level is huge. If you make a mistake you embarrass yourself in front of New York and maybe the world."

During *Live from Lincoln Center* broadcasts he plays on national TV, and during the orchestra's 2008 tour of North Korea, the concerts were broadcast around the world on TV and radio. "It's tough to travel and play. You're jet-lagged, disoriented, your whole body is screwed up. There's a reason athletes tend to lose on the road. Travel within the states is one thing, but try flying thirteen hours to China. Our job is to excel despite the circumstances."

The summer after he graduated from Northwestern he played more than fifty summer concerts before the regular season had even begun. The pace of learning and the range of repertoire force him to constantly learn new music and maintain familiarity with old music. The systematic preparation regimen he developed for the audition continues, in modified form, to define his preparation for concerts.

He sees many similarities between athletes and musicians: the motor control may be finer for musicians and the audience dressed differently, but both require stamina and attention to form in order to maintain a professional level. "I've always liked running, it's great for lung capacity and that's important for expanding your range of notes on the trumpet."

He also plays golf with a trombonist from the Philharmonic. In one sense it's a way to relax after the pressures of work, but it's also an application of the same skills in a different realm. "Golf takes a pretty unwavering focus and awareness of your body, and tiny adjustments can make a big difference in the outcome. Musicians are athletes, and especially for wind players, it's important to maintain good physical fitness. Lips are just muscles."

Beyond the physical challenges of staying in musical shape, he also faces the psychological work of staying calm in high-pressure situations. When Phil Smith got stuck in traffic once and called Matt at the last minute before a concert, he had to cover Phil's part. During a major solo in Ravel's *Bolero,* he struggled not to imagine all of the ways the solo could go wrong. "You have to fake the confidence, and you have to fake it so well that you convince yourself. I take deep breaths and don't think about the audience. Phil once told me, 'Just focus on playing the trumpet and everything else will take care of itself' and I realized that's the reason I'm here, because all I did is play the trumpet."

His work ethic is so ingrained now that even when he is relaxing, watching a baseball game or waiting for the train, he'll catch himself practicing complicated double or triple tonguing procedures. "I do worry about burnout. I hear stories of young people in good positions that don't end well. But I find I'm really busy in a good way. One week it's Beethoven, the next it's Stravinsky. There are so many amazing soloists and guest conductors, too. So I don't feel at risk of burnout because of the variety."

Another source of variety is his work with the New York Philharmonic Brass Quintet. The other four members are "some of the premier brass guys in the country, and three of them have been playing together for twenty-five years." To prepare for the recording of his first CD with the group, they rehearsed for up to five hours a day. He also toured as part of the ensemble. "One of the most interesting things was a Japan tour with the quintet. In the orchestra I'm not as featured, but in the quintet it's two hours of performing as just one of five players. So it's hugely taxing, but also extremely rewarding. We even had merchandise – mousepads and stickers. I'd only been in the orchestra a year and people in Japan were asking me to sign my photo on a mousepad."

The year after Matt joined the Philharmonic, another Northwestern trumpeter, Ethan Bensdorf, also won a seat in the orchestra. They were two of the youngest players ever to make it into the orchestra.

One night after a concert they were stopped by a young fan waiting outside the stage door. Matt was friendly and encouraging but also a bit surprised. Not long ago he had been a young fan of older players. "I met Wynton Marsalis in Sacramento in high school. I was blown away by the concert and I rushed backstage afterward and actually got to meet him. He just encouraged me to keep playing. Then after I joined the Philharmonic we had a joint concert with Jazz at Lincoln Center, and I got to play on the same stage with him. I don't think he remembered me, but I remembered him."

*Matt as a teenager with his pet donkey, Jasper*

*Matt in 2010 on a special From the Top episode featuring outstanding alumni*

photo credit: John Servies

photo credit: Caroline Cardiasmenos

# SECTION 3

## "Your Kids are Your Riches"

# Just a Lucky So-and-So

One day Dr. Haewon Moon, a teacher at the Duke Ellington School of the Arts, a high school in Washington DC, heard unusual sounds coming from the classroom near her office while she was eating lunch. "I heard these beautiful chords, and I followed the music and found one of my students playing. It was Clifton. I said 'Is that your own music?' He said 'No, I heard it on the radio this morning.' He can reproduce these complex harmonies perfectly. He has a beautiful ear."

Moon had been Clifton Williams' piano teacher for over a year, but she never realized he had the talent to play nearly anything after hearing it only once. She and Clifton worked together on classical repertoire, but his capacity for auditory recall was developed and perfected in the gospel music culture in which he was raised. Moon sensed that despite his musical talent, Clifton lacked confidence in his classical playing. After teaching at Duke Ellington for twenty years, she had often encountered a perception among many of her African-American students that classical music was "a realm for rich, white people. Of course it doesn't have to be. And students like Clifton disprove this stereotype. But I've seen my students wondering, 'Can I survive? Is it for black people?' My strategy is not to push. I just try to expose them and let them make a decision."

Clifton was introduced to gospel music when he was three. His mother took him to a gospel service at the church where she sang in the choir. "He just stared at the lady playin' piano, and once it was over he ran up and banged on the keys," she recalled. Clifton has a similar memory. "I remember being very young and hearing my grandma sing. This lady would play the piano and I'd always stalk her a little."

He played his first recital at the age of three on a small keyboard his grandmother got him. "I'd had two weeks of lessons and I had one song I could barely play. My mom gets loads of people to come and I'm sweating bullets. Of course as soon as I've finished she wants me to play it again. It was kind of awkward."

Ever since she was a girl, Clifton's mom has been called Peaches. "When I was born I looked like a Georgia peach, so that's what they called me." When she was a young girl, she wanted to be a famous singer. "I never tell nobody that, cause life took a different turn." When she had a baby at the age of fifteen, her hopes of musical fame vanished. "That was a big turn, when you become a mother, it's not so much about you, it's about us." She worked different low-wage jobs to make ends meet and for a while she managed a McDonalds. Shortly after Clifton was born, she had a dream in which he grew up to be a famous piano player. She hoped he would be able to have the musical career she never did.

When Clifton first started formal piano lessons at age nine, he had a reputation as a 'wild child'. "The teacher told me that Clifton was polite and well-mannered," Peaches recalled, "and I'd say, 'Girl, who you talkin' about? You just don't see him at home!' When he was young that boy'd rip and run and get into stuff. He used to win all the dance parties and if you messed with his little sister he'd fight. Nobody believes it because now he turned out to be the opposite."

Soon after his grandmother got him a keyboard, he began exploring as many different combinations of pitches and rhythms as he could imagine. At the age of seven he went to the Shirley Abrams Music Ministry, a school that trains young people in the traditions of gospel music. The school helped to focus his interest in music and gave him productive exercises to practice at home. "He always was self-motivated. Kids was like, 'Ms. Peaches, why your son don't come outside?' I said, 'I guess he don't want to.'" When Clifton was inside, he was generally playing the piano. "I used to get so annoyed when he played all the time, but gradually he started making sounds I could recognize."

Clifton's father, who was in and out of prison for most of Clifton's childhood, didn't initially understand his fascination with music. He once asked him, "Why don't you pick up a basketball or a football?" By the time he was a junior in high school, his father's attitude had changed. "Now he totally respects it," Clifton said as a high school junior. "He's seen me compete."

He made his first income from music at the age of eight. He earned twenty-five dollars for playing at a Sunday gospel service. By the time he was thirteen he was making significant money playing at church services. "I didn't know what a check was and I didn't care. My mom always told me, 'just pick one thing you love to do so when they don't pay you, you won't get so mad.'" His middle school years were the time when what he calls "the pre-busyness" started. He began playing more church gigs, he was competing in and winning various competitions, and he was still studying at the Shirley Abrams Gospel Ministry.

Moon first heard him play at the District of Columbia Public Schools Piano Competition. He was in seventh grade. "Everything was so right, the phrasing, dynamics, and tone quality," Moon thought as she listened to him play a short work by J.S. Bach. She approached him after his performance and suggested he audition for Duke Ellington the following year.

If middle school was a time of "pre-busyness," the era of full-fledged busyness began when he entered high school at Duke Ellington. A good deal of the busyness was caused by a simple problem: he didn't have a piano at home. As a younger pianist his talent and practice on a keyboard were sufficient to achieve considerable progress on the instrument. But as he became more advanced and began assuming more professional duties, the lack of an acoustic instrument at home was limiting his development. "Since he just played on a keyboard, he didn't have to develop wrist movement for articulation," said Moon. "This can affect your whole technique. I knew he was very talented, but he wasn't so sure of himself. He was very cautious – his goal when he began high school was just to get a music education degree and become a teacher."

One of the first pieces she assigned Clifton was Chopin's "Military" Polonaise, a piece that would help to develop his wrist strength and tone quality on an acoustic instrument. Since the piece was intended to develop precisely those skills that playing on an electronic keyboard could not, he tried to practice on the acoustic pianos at the high school as much as possible. Some days he came in before seven in the morning, other days he stayed late into the afternoon. Between after-school ensembles, practice for church gigs, and work on his classical repertoire, he was often at school for ten to twelve hours a day. His growing connections to multiple Baptist churches also gave him access to pianos on which he could practice.

Moon was so pleased by Clifton's progress on the Chopin "Polonaise" she encouraged him to apply to a prestigious festival through the Smithsonian, where he could perform the piece. She also printed out a copy of the *From the Top* application and urged him to apply. "He was scared, no confidence. I gave him the application but he didn't send it. His excuse was he didn't know he had to write an essay. He had other excuses for the festival, so he ended up not going to that, either.

Though Clifton may have been tentative in his initial explorations of classical music, his gospel career was flourishing. By the time he was sixteen, he was making roughly $20,000 a year by playing at churches around Washington DC and conducting multiple church choirs. His income from music allowed him to pay for his own food, clothing, and other expenses.

By his junior year, his schedule had intensified to the point that from Monday through Friday during the school year he left home at 7 A.M. and returned around 10 P.M. He also wanted to defend his academic class rank of first out of 130 students at Duke Ellington. Many weeks he was so busy with schoolwork and music that his sisters gave him a simple piece of advice: "you need to sit down, just sit down for a minute."

Though Clifton could drive himself to his gigs, trying to coordinate his and his mom's schedules with only one car was a constant challenge. "Every day my mom will compromise her schedule for mine. It's what I love her for. She wakes up and asks me where I need to be. She's really been there for me. She drops me off, she lets me use the car; she's always supportive. On a trip to Canada she was like, 'How 'bout I fly with you, then take the train back?'"

The Canada trip almost didn't happen. Clifton was supposed to travel to Niagara Falls for the induction of Shirley Adams, the woman who ran the music school he attended as a child, into the Gospel Hall of Fame. Despite setting an alarm, Clifton and Peaches both overslept. By the time they rushed over to get Clifton on the bus with his classmates, the bus had already left. So Peaches drove home and planned a road trip (Clifton talked her out of the plane/train idea.) "I got my cousin and my girlfriend and said 'Come on y'all, I'm takin' my baby to Canada.' We got lost like I don't know what, I got to cryin' and stuff. I didn't want to go on, but God showed me the way and we got him there that night. He didn't miss nothing."

♩ ♩ ♩

Clifton's work in gospel music called on different skills than classical playing. "It's common in Baptist churches for the choir not to use music. If they use music, they tend to look down at it so they forget to engage the audience. The choirs learn by ear, and so do I. I go to YouTube and listen to songs. When I hear it I can sit down and play it. Then maybe I transpose it or adapt it somehow to fit the needs of the choir."

The fact that the choir performs in the context of a church service also helps him to remember the larger function of the music. "You know, as musicians we feel the music is everything and that every little thing should be perfect. But on Sundays the music is there to inspire, encourage, and uplift people. We try to make the choir sound good because that inspires people. It's more about ministering through music than just playing music perfectly."

The music is so closely tied to its social and religious functions that improvisation is an essential skill for a gospel pianist. "After the sermon is brought forth, the minister will preach about this or that, and he'll request a particular song. We do so much improvising, just playing around in the moment, maybe a little background music during prayers to match the mood."

Just as Clifton will add improvised flourishes and chords to intensify a given mood, members of the congregation do a sort of improvisation as well. "People get involved. They don't just sit in the audience. They sing along, clap, stomp, shout out praise. They come to church stressed and bogged down. They need to escape from that negativity. Our job is to use music to help take them away from everything negative."

To experience what Clifton was describing, one Sunday I took the train to Washington DC and met him outside Pilgrim Rest Baptist Church in the Deanwood neighborhood of DC. Forged out of former slave plantations in the decades after the Civil War, Deanwood was one of the city's earliest African-American communities. The roads weren't paved until the 1960s, and the close-knit neighborhood maintained an old-fashioned texture well into the twentieth century.

The area has given rise to countless churches over the years. Just on the walk from the train to his church I passed the Fruit of the Spirit Church, the First Baptist Church, the Christian Fellowship, the New Birth Baptist Church, and the Prayer Missionary Baptist Church.

Clifton directs three choirs at Pilgrim Rest Baptist Church: the adult, the teenage, and the children's choir. He rehearses all three choirs every week and sometimes he'll squeeze in an extra practice before the first service on Sunday. On the morning I came to the church he was conducting a last-minute rehearsal with the children's choir. They were singing the classic gospel song, "Sometimes You Have to Encourage Yourself."

As he rehearsed the group, Clifton always seemed to be doing half a dozen things: asking the drummer to adjust his beat, handing the soloist a microphone, checking the lyrics to the second verse on his phone while giving an affirmative answer to the question, "Mr. Clifton, can I go to the bathroom?" The soloist was a nine-year-old girl who sang with striking confidence:

> Sometimes you have to encourage yourself
> Sometimes you got to speak victory
> During the test
> And no matter how you feel
> Speak the word and you will be healed
> Speak over yourself, encourage yourself in the Lord

After she sang through the song once, Clifton placed her hand on her stomach. "This is called your diaphragm," he said. "You want to feel this move while you sing." The girl nodded.

The next song they sang was called "Glory and Honor is Due Him." To teach the different vocal sections their parts, Clifton sang each voice line, leaping from baritone to a falsetto soprano and back again, all while supplying a harmonic framework with arpeggiated chords in his left hand. With his right hand he cued the entrances of each section and controlled the dynamic level of the ensemble. By raising his hand just a few inches higher the group instantly swelled to a greater volume.

The choir that morning was a mix of younger kids and teenagers. The two groups had merged for the annual neighborhood youth day the church was holding. They swayed to the beat of the music as they sang and when they finished a song the expressions on the singers' faces evoked the original meaning of the word gospel: good news. One boy was in such high spirits after a song that he danced his way down his row of the choir and proclaimed to no one in particular, "I'm goin' to the bathroom, yeah!"

Watching Clifton rehearse made clear just how intricate and demanding his job was. Every week he had to know every word and every note for every voice part for each song three different choirs were singing. Beyond knowing all of this himself, he also had to make sure everyone in the choir knew their words and music. He selected all the repertoire and worked to shape their expression and musicality. "It's gotten easier and also kind of harder," Clifton said of his work at Pilgrim Rest. "I'm used to directing, singing, and playing piano all at the same time. But it gets harder to find music that's right both musically and spiritually. You can't give young kids too many words or they'll forget them. So I try to look at the difficulty of the harmony, the number of words, whether there's a soloist, and if so whether any of the voices I have will be comfortable with it. Then I also consider the bigger picture of where the choir needs to go to grow as musicians. Sometimes I pick certain songs to help the choir understand something particular about harmony."

One thing that makes his job easier is the gift of total recall. "Right now it's become really easy. I can hear a song once and then sit down to play it and teach all of the parts. At this point, if I just sat down at a piano I could play gospel songs for two days straight without repeating one. Since I was little I've been hearing, playing, and singing this music. Now that it's also a job, you just got to know it on the spot. It helps that most gospel songs have shared formats, so you can learn the patterns and then lots of songs fit into them."

In middle school, Clifton used to practice transposing songs, scales, and chords into every possible key on the piano. He'd sit at his electric keyboard and start with simple sequences of chords in easier keys. Then as soon as he could play the patterns perfectly, he'd try harder harmonic progressions in more difficult keys. By the time he started high school he could transpose instantly and easily and soon he was using the skill every week as an accompanist and choir director.

While Clifton finished rehearsing the choir, members of the congregation began to arrive. One woman in a red dress stood in the aisle and encouraged the young soloist. "I can't hear you. Mama! Come on baby, open your mouth!" Clifton also tried to get the choir stirred up. "Listen to the words you're singing – 'I'm encouraged' – but you all sound a little broken, you've got to sound like it's true and you want to encourage someone else. I need y'all to give it all you got."

The service alternated between speech and song, prayer and music, and at any moment the congregation could participate. They chimed in throughout the sermon, sang or hummed along with the music during the songs, and came forth to the altar during prayers.

Near the end of the service the pastor gave a sort of community news bulletin – someone's wife's sister was not well, someone else had a cousin who just passed, another congregation member's mother was in the hospital after a heart attack. While he spoke Clifton improvised a soft series of held chords on electric organ. He watched and responded to the minister in almost the same way pianists would watch the screens of silent movies to craft the right mood to suit a scene.

The women in the congregation wore purple and yellow bandanas, flowered dresses, and straw hats with flowers slipped behind solid bands of dark cloth. The men wore suits, ties, and polished dress shoes. After a short prayer on the importance of family – "When the car is gone, the house is gone, all that's gone, family is all you have left" – people joined hands with their neighbors or kneeled in the aisles and prayed. Then Clifton and the young soloist from the choir performed, "Sometimes You Have to Encourage Yourself." Before she finished the first line of the first verse, people were muttering encouragement and clapping. Soon they began to rise and by the time the choir joined in the whole congregation was standing. Clifton played with his left hand and periodically snatched his right hand away from the keys to conduct and exhort the choir. They responded so seamlessly to his smallest motions they seemed like another instrument he was playing.

Most Sundays between services Clifton hurries home, drives his mom to work, and then rushes back. But that morning she had a rare day off, so Clifton was able to follow the congregation downstairs to the church basement, where long folding tables were heaped with platters of eggs, canned peaches, and sweet rolls. After breakfast, he still had to play a second service at Pilgrim Rest and services at two other churches.

♩ ♩ ♩

After Moon discovered Clifton's gift for reproducing whatever music he heard, she encouraged him to take AP Music Theory. He took the course his sophomore year in high school. Just as Moon expected, he had already grasped most of the material from his own practice and playing. He scored a five on the final, the highest possible score.

The lack of confidence she sensed in Clifton as a freshman also seemed to be changing. He'd aced an AP test, gotten steady work in various churches, and made quick progress in challenging classical repertoire. "She was a great encourager," Clifton said of Moon. "She was more than a teacher, more of a mentor. I really liked her. She always left room for me to expand my knowledge."

"The first thing he said to me in eleventh grade was, 'I want to play for *From the Top*,'" Moon said. He also began playing in more competitions. He sent in an audition CD to *From the Top* with a recording of Prokofiev's "Diabolical Suggestion," a tricky showpiece he'd been working on since his freshman year. He was accepted for a show in Boston in March. It was the latest of several trips he and his mom made for his music. "I'd never been outside DC before Clifton became involved in music," Peaches told me. "Bein' with Cliff I get to travel a lot. I play the numbers sometimes but God told me your kids are your riches. And I believe that."

Clifton and his mom drove to Boston the night before the show and arrived in time for a pizza party with the other performers,

Christopher O'Riley and a few members of the *From the Top* staff. The purpose of the pizza party, according to *From the Top* music producer Tom Vignieri, is to release nervous energy and help the kids get to know one another. Clifton met a cellist, flutist, and harpist, and after pizza and Cokes, each of the kids ran through their piece for the small gathering.

The show the following day was taped live at New England Conservatory's Jordan Hall before a packed house of one thousand. It featured *From the Top*'s signature blend of humor, interviews, and performances. While setting up his laptop on the piano, O'Riley turned to the crowd and gestured at the laptop he uses to display his music. "So I can watch basketball," he said. While the skeleton of the show is typically scripted, these are the sorts of improvisations that lend it a particular charm. Also seemingly improvised was Executive Producer Jerry Slavet dancing across the stage as the show opened to the sound of James Brown's "I Feel Good."

Clifton was getting more comfortable performing for large crowds, but he found a national radio audience intimidating. Before he walked onstage to play, he told himself the following: "God please get me through this and I'll never do it again." He made one slight slip in his performance of the Prokofiev, but overall he was pleased with how he played, and the audience loved it. He also played a second time on the program, accompanying the members of the Boston Children's Chorus on the song, "Bridge Over Troubled Water."

After his appearance on *From the Top*, the show's staff encouraged *The Washington Post* to write a feature on him. As a result of the story, which revealed that he didn't own an acoustic piano, several people offered to donate pianos so he could practice at home. Clifton also received one of *From the Top*'s Jack Kent Cooke Awards, a $10,000 scholarship for accomplished young musicians who have financial need.

In May of his junior year, Moon arranged for Clifton and some of her other students to perform at the Steinway Gallery on 57th Street in New York City, just a block away from Carnegie Hall. When they arrived at the gallery, the kids accepted an employee's invitation to try any of the instruments and fanned out across the second floor.

Soon the mingled sounds of a dozen songs filled the gallery. "I gotta get me a Steinway," one boy said after playing a few chords.

Clifton found an automatic player piano and started pressing buttons, which made the keys play themselves. "You could so scare somebody at your house with this," he said.

While the kids were in New York City, Moon took them on tours of various colleges and conservatories. "I want the kids to see as many colleges as possible, otherwise they think that this is somebody else's story," she said. Over the years, she's had students take many different directions. Some dropped out of high school and got into drugs, others went on to conservatories. One became so successful in the gospel world that when she jokingly asked him when he'd make his first million, he told her that it shouldn't be too long now. After a snack of raisins, nuts, juice, and cookies in a pink-walled-room on the second floor, the kids made their way down to the central atrium of the gallery.

A chandelier hung from the domed ceiling, white marble columns flecked with green veins were recessed in the walls, and electric candles cast an orange glow over a large, stormy portrait of Franz Schubert. The evening crowds were rushing past on 57th Street, but five rows of steel folding chairs easily accommodated the sparse audience that had assembled.

After an expressive and precise performance of a Chopin scherzo, Clifton shot up from the piano bench as soon as he touched the last note, wiped his forehead with the back of his hand, and smiled at the audience. "Phew," he said.

While Clifton was practicing on a mahogany baby grand that afternoon, he interspersed gospel chords and a stylish rendition of Duke Ellington's "I'm Just a Lucky So-and-So," with passages of the Chopin scherzo.

He hopes to maintain this musical versatility throughout his life. "I really admire someone like Wynton Marsalis, doing a collaboration with Lang Lang, or Herbie Hancock playing Mozart." He pictures his future as a geographically expanded version of the present. Rather than running between churches and performances in the DC area, he hopes that he'll be, "running from country to country for different concerts." He wants to improve his jazz, gospel, and classical playing. In jazz and gospel he's trying to improvise with smoother phrasing. "I absolutely love to improvise, to do the unexpected thing, you know, to play the chord no one will expect, not cause it's wrong just cause it's different. But it can be a challenge to do that in real time." He also wants to expand his classical repertoire and to win some major competitions. Moon loaned him a documentary about the Van Cliburn Competition and he's been interested ever since. "Maybe I'll win the Van Cliburn, that would be good."

Though his ambitions are great, Clifton often reminds himself of some advice he once got from Thelonious Monk, Jr. at a reception. "Monk said that connections and love matter more than technique." The advice reminded me of something a woman at the Pilgrim Rest Congregation told the nine-year-old soloist before she sang. "If you sing it with joy, if you ministerin' to me with joy, I'm gonna be encouraged."

*Clifton in Austria performing for the US Ambassador to Vienna*

*Clifton at seventeen performing on From the Top*

*Clifton rehearsing with his class in preparation for high school graduation*

*Clifton, the class valedictorian, poses with his parents at graduation*

# It was Pianos Everywhere

When she was a girl in Ukraine in the 1960s, Natasha Bukhart-seva saw an ancient upright piano in a dusty corner of her school's auditorium. She asked her parents to buy a piano, but they told her it would be too dangerous. There were Soviet agents stationed in each village who looked for signs of disloyalty to the Communist party. The well-educated and cultured were regarded with particular suspicion in an era when official ideology celebrated the "common man." There was also the constant threat neighbors would report you to the authorities, either to settle a grudge or curry favor. In such a climate of fear and mistrust, they felt the worst thing they could do was to make the family more conspicuous, even by doing something as simple as buying an upright piano.

Twenty years before, Natasha's grandfather had disappeared one night. He was a well-educated lawyer with an affinity for music and the arts, which made him vulnerable to Soviet suspicions. The family never heard what happened to him, but assumed that, like thousands of other Ukrainians, he was murdered under the Stalinist regime.

Ever since she had been unable to play piano as a girl, Natasha had always wanted her own daughter to play. At twenty, Natasha left her village to study at a meat college in Pskov, near the Russian-Estonian border. She learned how to examine, process, handle, and prepare different kinds of meat. The work was hardly glamorous, but it seemed stable, gave her enough to eat, and removed any grounds for suspicion. After four years in Pskov she moved to Odessa, where she met her future husband. They were married in 1990, just as the Soviet Union was collapsing.

Her daughter, Dasha, was born in August, 1992. After the official collapse of the Soviet Union in 1991, Ukraine declared independence and enjoyed a brief moment of euphoria: the political and psychological nightmare of Soviet oppression was finally over. But after a half-century as a Soviet satellite state, the country lacked a basic infrastructure and stable economy. There was no national currency, and crime and chaos began to engulf major cities like Odessa. Natasha still had a job at a meat processing plant, but she was paid in government-issued coupons, a makeshift currency that was counterfeited, hoarded, and subject to wild depreciation.

She and her husband lived with Dasha and several other poor families in a condemned house without running water or electricity. Their house was falling apart – the wallpaper was stained and peeling, the doors were missing hinges, the floorboards were rotted and warped. Depressed and jobless, her husband began vanishing for days at a time, only to return reeking of vodka. One night, Natasha woke to the sounds of creaking wood and low whispering voices coming from Dasha's room. She crept to the open door and saw two thieves scouring the room for valuables. She started screaming and they leapt out the first-floor window and ran down the street. She and Dasha were unharmed and nothing had been stolen, but she knew they'd been lucky. Violent robberies were occurring all around the city.

The episode prompted her to move with Dasha back to Vishniyaki, a rural village where her father, sister, grandmother, and a cousin shared a small house. They raised pigs, chickens, geese, and ducks and kept two dogs and three cats. In the field surrounding the house they grew carrots, potatoes, cabbages, corn, and other crops. Food was scarce and there was never any extra money for amenities. But the house in Vishniyaki did have one advantage – an old, out-of-tune piano in the living room that had been gathering dust ever since Natasha's sister got it from the local school in the early 1980s.

From an early age, Dasha was fascinated by the instrument. "I felt it was the thing I'd do all my life," Dasha told me. As soon as she could walk, she would toddle over to it, open the lid, and bang on the keys. She was content to sit for long stretches of time and make whatever sounds she could.

For most of the year the adults worked outside and Dasha would sit with her great-grandmother next to a wood-burning stove in the living room. Dasha's earliest memories are among her fondest. She spent her days listening to her great-grandmother's stories, playing with the family's cats and dogs, and teaching herself to play simple songs.

Life was harder for Natasha. The animals and the garden provided barely enough to eat, and there was still the rent and electricity to pay each month. Natasha's sister worked at a factory and made just enough to cover the electric bill. But Natasha had no way to make money in Vishniyaki, so she began doing what many unemployed Ukrainians did: traveling to Moscow to sell things on the streets. She took a thirty-six hour train ride to Moscow, riding in the cheapest, most crowded compartment and sleeping and eating in her seat. Sore and exhausted, she arrived in Moscow and sold packets of sugared almonds and cashews on the streets. To avoid paying the cost of a hotel, she slept on sidewalk benches and in train stations, then took her bags of nuts and spent another day on the streets hawking them. It was only barely profitable. She spent the bulk of her earnings on the return train ticket, so her net profit was negligible. But without her small contributions the family would not have been able to pay the rent.

Dasha started at the village school when she was six. Her great-grandmother had already taught her to read words, and at school she learned to read notes on the keyboard, and sang folk songs with the other children. "I would ride my bike home from school and practice reading the names on signs," Dasha said.

But one day she came home from school to find her mother gone. Her great grandmother told her that her mother needed to go away.

The longest Dasha and her mother had ever been separated was a handful of days. But Natasha was no longer making any money from the trips to Moscow. More and more Ukrainians were selling goods on the streets and the market was saturated. A friend of her sister's had a room in her Odessa apartment, and Natasha thought she would be able to get her old job back at the processing plant. The family desperately needed money, so she left for Odessa.

The processing plant told her that her old job had been filled. She returned day after day, usually waiting for eight hours in a crowded room only to speak a few sentences to an indifferent bureaucrat. She told each person she needed the job to feed her daughter. Finally someone listened – after almost three weeks she was given a job.

She made the equivalent of twenty dollars a month. The low wages and the high cost of train tickets made it impossible to visit Dasha more than once every few months. When she did, she saved money by taking an overnight train that arrived at 4 A.M. Dasha always promised herself she would stay awake for the arrival, but Natasha always found Dasha asleep in her aunt's arms.

Dasha missed her mom between visits, but she had school and loving relatives. For Natasha, the time was more difficult. She worked long hours only to return to a tiny apartment she shared with six strangers. The apartment was unheated and all through the winter she was perpetually shivering. Phone calls were prohibitively expensive, so she had to choose between calling Dasha frequently or visiting her.

After two years, Natasha decided she couldn't live apart from her daughter. She found a ten by ten foot room in Odessa, and Dasha left her village life to join her mom there. It was the summer before she began third grade. She was eight years old.

They lived in a building constructed in the 1950s under Khrushchev's program to standardize housing. Like many American public housing projects, the buildings in Odessa were initially clean and well-maintained, but fell into disrepair after years of neglect. By the year 2000, when Dasha and Natasha moved in, the steel on the exterior was rusted and exposed, whole chunks of faded concrete were crumbling, and graffiti was scrawled on the walls.

They lived on the first floor and to get to the apartment they walked down a long hallway that was nearly pitch black even during the day. An occasional bulb hung from the ceiling, making sputtering sounds. The only running water was in a common bathroom at the end of the hallway. They did dishes, laundry, and took baths in a tub in the common bathroom.

Odessa was full of commotion and crime; every day Dasha saw something she'd never seen before. One day, she and her mom were outside beating the dust off their blankets when they saw two women walking back from the outdoor market. A man approached the women and asked them the time. While one woman was looking at her watch he grabbed her necklace, ripped it from her neck and ran. A few days later, while riding on a bus, they saw the same man staring intently at their wrists and hands, trying to appraise the value of their jewelry. They had nothing of great value, but they waited until he got off the bus and walked home from a different stop.

On weekends, Dasha went with her mom to a vast open-air market where hundreds of vendors were arrayed in snaking rows of tents and stalls. They sold fish, potatoes, pork, beef, milk, shoes, jeans, earrings, fur coats, and stolen cell phones, among other things. Natasha wandered through the entire market, searching for the lowest price on a loaf of bread or a pound of beef, haggling with the vendors until she got a good price.

In October, Dasha began piano lessons at the age of eight. Natasha didn't think music was something Dasha would do professionally, but she thought it would enrich her life and distract her from some of the crime and poverty in Odessa. She'd heard of a good piano teacher at the music school from a friend and managed to leave work early one afternoon to take Dasha to audition. Since Dasha had no formal training, the audition was brief. The teacher asked Dasha to sing increasingly complex sequences of notes to gauge the quality of her ear and musical memory. Dasha could sing whatever patterns the teacher played. They started lessons the following week.

"My first teacher was the most amazing person in the world. She loved music and gave every part of herself to music," Dasha told me. She was always eager to practice, but finding a piano was difficult. Crammed in their room was the single bed they shared, all of their clothing, a few simple cooking items, and a battered black-and-white TV with tinfoil wrapped around its antenna to enhance the signal. Even if they could afford a piano, there was nowhere to put it.

Dasha had a piano lesson twice a week. She left school at 3 P.M. and took a bus – a private minivan with eight to ten people piled inside – across Odessa to the music school. Traffic was always terrible and the roads were gutted with gaping potholes. After an hour of bumpy progress she got off in the neighborhood near the meat processing plant. It wasn't a safe area; there were rows of abandoned houses in which homeless men and petty thieves drank vodka, and the streets were strewn with garbage and the collapsed forms of drunken men. In the fall and winter it was already dark by five, so Natasha met Dasha at the bus and the two hurried through the derelict streets in the fading afternoon light.

The music school was an oasis in the midst of desolation. Dasha would arrive and lose herself in music for a few hours before venturing back into the cold. Her teacher opened a studio that was supposed to remain locked and let Dasha play before and after her one hour lesson. The walls were thin enough, and her teacher's ears acute enough, that Dasha would hear her teacher call out corrections and advice through the walls – less pedal! That should be a B-flat! – even while teaching another pupil in her own studio.

Dasha made quick progress, but playing only two days a week limited her development. They still couldn't afford a piano, and Natasha couldn't leave work early more than twice a week to escort Dasha to the music school. So Natasha improvised. She rummaged through a supply room at work and found a long, poster-size sheet of blank white paper. She cut it in two and taped the halves together to extend the length. Then she drew six equally spaced black lines and further divided the white space to create eight white keys and five black keys.

Dasha was delighted. "I loved that paper keyboard," she said. She set the paper keyboard on the side of the bed, sat on the floor and played by the dim light of the single, dirty bulb that illuminated their room. The unusual practice method forced her to develop a strong capacity to hear music in her head simply by looking at notes on a page.

After only a few months of lessons, Dasha's teacher suggested she try a competition. It was hosted by the music school where she studied and was held in their main auditorium. She began practicing more intensely. She stayed up until midnight or later, practicing passages on the paper piano. Natasha often dozed off while Dasha was still practicing. The last image she saw before closing her eyes was the focused face of her daughter seated on the floor, a score spread open above the paper keyboard.

The competition took place on a cold Saturday. Students from music schools around the country filed into the main auditorium with their parents and teachers. Dasha was so nervous her whole body trembled. She'd only played for her mom and her teacher, now she faced a packed auditorium. After a quick warm-up, she waited backstage with her mom until she heard her name called. As she sat down on the piano bench, she realized her legs barely touched the floor and that her right leg was shaking uncontrollably, which made it difficult to maneuver the piano pedals.

She played two simple pieces – one by Bach and one by Mozart – and to her surprise she remembered them and made no mistakes. She was jolted from the musical trance by the sound of applause as she hurried offstage to join her mom and teacher in the audience. Late in the afternoon, the judges walked onstage and announced five winners, one from each age group. She won first prize for the youngest group.

Dasha began competing more and traveling to other cities around Ukraine. After she won first prize at several other competitions, her teacher waived her tuition at the music school. Her teacher also began coming to competitions in other cities to help coach Dasha before the events. Natasha always tried to pay for the teacher's train ticket and food as a token of her gratitude. To economize, Natasha brought food from Odessa that they could eat during the trips. Usually, they ate thick whole wheat bread with animal fat, a common filling meal eaten all over Ukraine.

"At first music was just for fun, just to be familiar with it, then at competitions I knew it was my life," Dasha said, "and I realized there was no way back."

Dasha loved competing; music mingled in her mind with the adventure and excitement of overnight train rides to new towns and cities. She'd fall asleep nestled between her mom and her teacher and awaken in the morning as the train chugged into a new place.

On competition days, it seemed as though her teacher took away Dasha's nerves and assumed them herself. While she could practice and prepare with Dasha, she could never bring herself to listen to her perform in a competition. Instead, she would pace in the corridors with clenched fists until the event was over. As soon as Dasha and Natasha met her in the lobby, she would rush up to them, hug

Dasha, then ask, "Did they applaud?" "Of course," Dasha told her. "Mom was the loudest!"

♪ ♪ ♪

The winner of a series of competitions within Ukraine was automatically qualified for a major competition in Paris. Most of the other kids competing in Dasha's age group had been playing longer and were able to practice more than Dasha. But she continued winning events until one day she qualified for the Paris competition. Natasha and Dasha were thrilled, but paying for plane tickets and a hotel room seemed impossible.

The director of the competition asked Natasha for a fax number so he could send her details about the event. Though she wasn't supposed to receive personal faxes at work, she gave him the number at the processing plant. A few weeks later, a friend handed her a sheaf of papers. She pored through them, and felt a rush of pride to see Dasha's name on the list of competitors. During her lunch break she took the papers over to a municipal office building to show some friends. Just as she got there, a reporter arrived to interview a wealthy businessman at the building. After Natasha told her friends about the competition, they told the reporter, who told the businessman. In a matter of minutes, he promised them money for plane tickets from Odessa to Paris.

Natasha returned to work with a check from one of Ukraine's wealthiest businessmen. She didn't have a way to pay for a hotel room, but she booked two plane tickets anyway. It was Dasha's first time on a plane and she spent the flight in a state of fear mingled with excitement. She stared out at the shapes of clouds, but she couldn't keep her mind from conjuring images of planes plummeting from the sky.

They arrived in Paris and, with a few French phrases, managed to navigate the public transit system to the neighborhood of the conservatory hosting the competition. "Paris seemed like something from a fairytale, the streets and buildings were all so perfect," Dasha said. But Natasha was growing anxious about paying for a hotel. She started imagining being arrested in Paris and languishing in a dingy French prison. She thought maybe they could sleep in a park or on a bus that looped around the city, but she couldn't bring herself to tell Dasha there was no money for a hotel.

Before she had more time to worry, Dasha tugged her across a busy street and into the beautiful, marble-floored hotel lobby. Dasha walked up to the counter and asked for a room in English, one of the languages she studied at school. To Natasha's surprise, the clerk reached across the counter and handed Dasha a key. She said a few words in English and Dasha translated for her mom: "Sign now, pay later."

It was Dasha's first time competing without her teacher, and the new language and unfamiliar city made even finding a practice room a challenge. Natasha brought some canned beans and fruit and the usual bread with animal fat, and after breakfast on the morning of the competition they ventured out to look for a piano. They were turned away from several music schools and had no choice but to make their way to the competition without warming up.

The first place prize was 450 euros, far more than Dasha had ever won before and more than enough to cover the cost of the hotel. The rounds of the competition were closed to the public. Natasha waited in the lobby, watching each performance on a small TV.

Dasha advanced through the preliminary rounds in the morning, and after a quick lunch of bread and fruit she was ready for the afternoon's finals. Natasha was pacing in the lobby, hardly able to glance at the TV screen showing the performances. After a few hours, the screen went dark and Dasha joined her mom and a swelling crowd in the lobby. Natasha was thinking of escape routes from the hotel: back doors, windows, any exit so they could slip out without paying. She couldn't stand the thought of having to tell Dasha, and she was also afraid of what could happen if they were caught.

But before she had more time to worry, people were surrounding and congratulating her. She didn't understand their French, but the message of the judges who shook her hands was clear: Dasha had won first prize.

With the rest of their time they went to the top of the Eiffel Tower and looked out over Paris. They could see the Louvre, l'Arc De Triomphe, everything. They used the aerial view to chart a course for the rest of the day and spent their last hours in Paris visiting famous monuments and museums. The next morning they went down to the hotel lobby, paid the bill, and flew home.

᠊᠊᠊ ᠊᠊᠊ ᠊᠊᠊

In August of 2000, Dasha's grandfather passed away and they went back to Vishniyaki for the funeral. When they returned to Odessa, they found they had no place to live. "They'd thrown away all our food and our stuff was in boxes," Dasha said. "We slept on chairs in the lobby that night, but we were hiding; we had nowhere to live." The landlord of the building had given their room to one of his family members and they would have to move out in a matter of days.

The landlord was unmoved by their pleas to stay. Natasha asked friends and family for leads on apartments, but with so little notice nothing turned up. There was always the option of squatting in an abandoned or condemned home, but Natasha's memory of her first year with Dasha in Odessa was enough to dissuade her. With nowhere else to turn, they went to the director of Dasha's music school and explained their predicament. She offered to let them sleep in a classroom until they could find other lodgings.

The room was more of a studio than a classroom. The walls were covered with yellow flowered wallpaper and the floor was dirty, scuffed linoleum. There were two tables, a grand piano, and a few chairs. They cooked on a small, three-legged electric hot plate on the table that became their kitchen. The other table was their bedroom, where they slept and stored their clothes. "The worst thing was there was no bathroom," said Dasha. "There was a toilet and sink, but the problem was to bathe. In the back of the school was a little garden behind tall bushes, where nobody could see us. So we boiled water and washed there."

The director of the school was risking her job by letting them live there, so they had to be secretive. Dasha met her mom at work after school and the two waited there until 7 P.M. or later, when they knew most of the lessons and classes had finished. Then they would walk quickly through the dark streets and let themselves quietly into the school. It was inevitable some people knew they were living there, but whenever they cooked or talked or moved about they had to be as silent as possible. If the wrong person discovered them there, they could easily end up on the streets.

They whispered and crept about the room until late at night, when they could finally be sure everyone had gone home. At that point, the music school became their own. "It was pianos everywhere," Dasha said. While she practiced, Natasha cooked the meals for the next day on the small hot plate. Sometime after midnight, they both fell asleep on the hard, narrow table they shared.

In the mornings, they had to be furtive once again and on weekends they had to stay out of the room for the entire day. "We woke at 5 A.M. to avoid being discovered," Dasha said. Every hint of habitation had to be carefully cleaned, removed or concealed. This gave their temporary shelter a feeling of terrible fragility. They couldn't ever unpack or settle in, and when they returned in the evenings they'd find evidence of the heavy use the room had received in the dirt on the floor, the stray forgotten papers on the tables, and the occasional wad of chewing gum stuck to the wood where they'd sleep that night.

One Saturday morning, Dasha was slower than usual in tidying the room and a little girl arrived early for her piano lesson. The girl opened the door to the room and Dasha froze halfway through folding a blanket. Pots and the electric hot plate were still on the kitchen table and two open suitcases were visible on the floor. The girl was around seven, three years younger than Dasha. At first she was confused, then fascinated. "That's so cool! I want to live here too," she said. She told Dasha she loved building forts in her house out of tables and chairs and blankets and pretending she lived in them. Dasha realized the girl was too small to understand she and her mother had not moved to the music school in order to build forts and play make-believe. She let the girl chatter on for a few minutes, then told her, "Maybe we can switch homes – I'll go stay in your apartment and you can live here." The girl nodded excitedly and ran off.

The reality of living in the room was far from the idyllic adventure the girl had imagined. As the fall deepened and the weather turned colder, the temperature in the room dropped as well. They bundled up in sweaters and blankets, but there was still the problem of bathing outside in frigid temperatures. Natasha's back had begun to ache from sleeping on the hard wooden table and bathing outside exacerbated the pain to the point that she could barely move. The pain could make her lose her job, and without job or home they'd join the thousands of starving homeless who lived and died on the streets. Her nerves and anxiety also exacerbated her back pain. The pain caused her to worry, and her worries worsened her pain. Often the pain was so severe Natasha lay down while Dasha did the cooking. "Mom's back pain was so bad I had to feed her with a spoon as she was lying down," Dasha said. After dinner she would clean up the dishes, clear a space on the table, and start her homework, taking frequent breaks to practice piano.

At first she'd been happy: we have a place to stay, she thought, so what's there to worry about? She was surrounded by pianos and playing more than ever. But as she saw her mother becoming more and more anxious, the feelings started to transfer to Dasha. "I was nervous because my mom was nervous all the time." Even years later, it's hard for Dasha to talk about her time at the music school. "Once I had an interview in Odessa with a journalist and they asked me about living in the music school and I wept. That was the end of the interview."

Just as late fall turned to winter, Natasha found them a room in a hostel. It was small and they shared it with another woman, but anything was an improvement compared to the music school. As they settled in, Dasha noticed her mother had changed. She'd always been nervous, but now the slightest thing – a small fluctuation in the price of food – could trigger intense, uncontrollable anxieties. And even worse, since they'd left the music school, Dasha no longer had a place to practice every day.

Two solutions to this problem soon emerged. Natasha always asked people she knew and even some she didn't if they had an old piano they didn't want. One day on a bus she asked an older gentleman who said yes, she was welcome to his old piano. Natasha and Dasha wheeled it themselves along miles of bumpy, cracked sidewalks, and placed it in the common room of their new hostel. The jostling and jarring of moving hadn't helped the tuning of the piano. Once in place, it made the clangy, discordant sound of pianos played in old westerns.

The other residents of the hostel weren't pleased by the addition of a piano to the common room. Many nights Dasha's practicing was punctuated by the sounds of people kicking the wall behind the piano. But despite the distraction of kicks and curses, she focused intently on the music, burrowing her way inside a piece until all distractions disappeared.

The other solution came from Natasha's meat-processing plant. Many older facilities still had auditoriums that were vestiges of the Soviet era. Once used for party rallies and ceremonies, they now sat vacant. One day during a lunch break, Natasha wandered into a different wing of the plant, opened a door and discovered a cavernous, cold room with a piano in one corner. She brought Dasha the next day and let her practice there. The piano was in better condition than the one in the hostel, but winter had arrived and the auditorium was entirely unheated. The temperature in the room hovered in the teens and twenties, just above the temperature outside. Dasha bundled herself in heavy coats, scarves and hats, but her fingers would quickly grow sluggish and lose agility if she played for more than a few minutes. So she tried different pairs of gloves until she found a pair thin enough not to impede the motion of her fingers but thick enough to provide some warmth.

Dasha was starting to make money playing music. After winning the competition in Paris and several more in Ukraine, the Ukrainian government awarded Dasha a monthly stipend of about twenty-five dollars for being a "gifted child." Six months later, she played at a luncheon for successful businesswomen in Odessa. One of the women ran a travel agency and tour company and sometimes arranged concerts for tourists. She invited Dasha to play at these events. Each concert earned her about fifty dollars and she also sold DVDs and CDs of herself playing. The extra money helped her mom meet expenses and even allowed for occasional treats like ice cream or a new blouse.

♪ ♪ ♪

Dan and Lynne Levinson didn't consider themselves philanthropic. Since their retirement in 2005, they've visited over ninety countries. They jointly ran a construction company for thirty years before they built their dream house in Aspen, Colorado and retired, planning to travel for the rest of their lives.

In September, 2006, they were on a cruise on the Black Sea. The last stop on their itinerary was in Kiev, where they heard a concert featuring Dasha. They were struck by the juxtaposition of her small figure and the powerful sounds she produced. "She was this tiny thing, only fourteen," Dan recalled, "and she blew everyone's socks off." After the concert they congratulated Dasha. They chatted for a couple of minutes and told her there was a famous music festival in Aspen, where they lived. Dan asked Dasha if she would like to come there to play piano. He'd posed the question flippantly, not expecting she would take him seriously. But as soon as he spoke, her eyes brightened and fixed on his. "When do we go and what do I play?" she asked.

Dan and Lynne discussed what to do, but the decision seemed to have made itself. The more they learned about Dasha's story and the more they got to know her, the more they wanted to help. "You shouldn't offer something unless you mean it," said Dan. "We thought if we could actually help this little girl, we should."

They began to coordinate the details of bringing Dasha and Natasha across the world to spend the summer at their home in Aspen. Dan showed a DVD of Dasha playing to the admissions faculty of the Aspen Music Festival and they agreed to waive the requirement of a live audition.

In April, 2007 Dan flew back to Odessa to help Dasha and Natasha get visas. Dozens of Ukrainians claimed to have host families or jobs waiting for them in America, and Dasha would have had trouble convincing the relevant officials without Dan to corroborate her story. During his trip, Dan was deeply moved when he saw the hostel and the music school where they had lived. As they told him about the precarious nature of housing in Odessa, he realized that leaving the room for eight weeks to go to Aspen meant losing it permanently. Even if they paid for the room, the landlord would simply rent it to someone else and double his profit. "I knew that as long as they were renting they could be kicked out," Dan said.

He called Lynne. "How do you feel about owning a house in Odessa?"

"What?! Are you crazy?" she said.

With a bit of persuading, she saw his point of view. "We knew it was the right thing to do. It's so easy not to do something," Dan said. "Doing something is hard and convoluted and really expensive, but you've got to do it." By committing to host them for the summer, the Levinsons became more deeply involved than they expected. It wasn't exactly how he'd envisioned retirement, but Dan attacked each new obstacle until finally all the paperwork was in order, the documents signed, and the house was theirs. "It was bizarre," he said. "I hired lawyers, translators, and I had to fly back and fill out papers to authorize them to stay there, and the papers had to be notarized in Russian."

In June, 2007, Dasha and Natasha flew to New York, where they met Dan and Lynne and continued to Denver en route to Aspen.

When Natasha first heard that a couple from a place called Aspen wanted to host her and Dasha for an entire summer she was incredulous. It seemed too good to be true. She thought maybe they only intended to pay for plane tickets and she and Dasha would have to find food and housing on their own. She also had darker suspicions; human smuggling and kidnapping weren't unheard of in Odessa. She arrived with a wad of Ukrainian money stashed in her sock that she borrowed from friends as a safeguard against the possibility the Levinsons were human traffickers. By the end of the summer she seemed somewhat less fearful, but since her English was limited to "hello," "thank you" and "good," it was hard to know how she felt.

Dasha was thrilled by what she saw on the drive from Denver to Aspen. She kept exclaiming, "This is unbelievable!" There were so many new things to absorb – the taste of a buffalo burger, the smoothness of the roads, the sight of mountains covered by green aspen trees, the massive size of stores like Costco. "Aspen is unlike anything in Ukraine, and everything was new and different," she said. "Living with people you barely know, who take care of you; having breakfast, lunch, and dinner with them; and even the food is totally different. The bread in America is worse."

Over the next few weeks, she found she also had many new musical ideas to assimilate. Because she'd spent so much time practicing on a paper keyboard, her wrists weren't used to holding the position necessary for producing a good tone on an piano with weighted keys. She had to relearn many basic skills – scales, chords, arpeggios – using a new technique. She also encountered dozens of other young pianists at or beyond her level, something she wasn't used to.

She practiced on the Levinson's baby grand piano in their living room, looking out at the mountains. "Once I looked up and there was a deer eating the bushes in the yard," she said.

Although they'd gone from poverty in Odessa to the luxury of Aspen, their situation felt very precarious. "We were afraid to wake up," said Dasha. "It seemed like a dream." They were in the United

States only because of the kindness of two strangers. Their long-term future was very uncertain, and the Levinsons couldn't support them forever.

As she took weekly lessons with a professor from the Peabody Conservatory, Dasha discovered many problems with her technique that resulted from her erratic access to decent pianos. Some of the American students played difficult passages so effortlessly it seemed miraculous. Dasha had to practice slowly and pay attention to tiny details that had been subconscious. Little by little she began to develop new habits and an awareness of the problems with some of her old habits.

A highlight of the summer was her appearance on *From the Top*, taped at the Aspen Music Festival. The show featured her playing two Ukrainian pieces, Vitaly Filipenko's "Toccata" and Oleg Polevoy's "Autumn Leaves." Dasha also told the audience she was enjoying her visit to Aspen. "I like to watch the mountains through the window in the morning when I'm practicing," she said.

As the summer progressed, she got to know the Levinsons better. One evening she even cooked them borscht – a soup of cabbage, beets, tomato, and beef served with hot white bread dipped in oil and garlic.

When Dasha and Natasha returned to Ukraine after the eight-week festival, they lived in a home of their own – no landlord could evict them, no music students could barge in on them. It was small, but located in a relatively safe area made even safer by a tall perimeter wall with chips of broken glass embedded on top to discourage thieves. Dan and Lynne were already discussing plans to bring them back for the next summer as well.

Dasha stayed in touch with the Levinsons via phone and email, and halfway through the year they called and asked if she'd like to stay in America and go to school after the upcoming summer festival at Aspen. They thought she'd have a better shot at succeeding if she studied with the best teachers in the United States. "We never expected we'd be doing this in our retirement. Even once we brought Dasha and Natasha over for the first summer, there was no clear long-term plan, we just made it up as we went along and tried to do the right thing," Dan said.

The Levinsons began to raise money among their friends to pay for an apartment in New York City and tuition to the Professional Children's School in Manhattan. Even though Dasha would have already finished high school in Ukraine, they wanted to give her another year to adjust to America, learn English, and prepare for auditions at American conservatories. In the spring of 2008, the Levinsons wrote to Dasha and Natasha with good news; they would spend the summer in Aspen, then move to an apartment on the Upper West Side of Manhattan. Dasha would go to high school, apply to conservatories, and study at Juilliard's pre-college division.

The Levinsons were convinced the only way Dasha had a chance of a career as a pianist was by studying with the best teachers in the United States. Between tuition, rent, and food, they had to pay almost $3,000 a month. "If we had tried to plan ahead, we wouldn't be doing what we are today. We've just tried to improvise as we go," Dan said. They had to travel less and fundraise more, but they were committed to giving Dasha the best possible chance for a career in music.

Dasha's friends in Odessa were excited for her: "My friend, Dasha," said one, "You are going to America, you need to find me a husband there."

They left Odessa in June, 2008, unsure if they would ever return. From the beginning of her second summer at the Aspen Music Festival, Dasha was focused on auditions at Juilliard in New York and Peabody in Baltmore, both scheduled for early 2009. Acceptance would not only mean the chance to study with a renowned teacher, it would also mean a student visa and four more years in the United States. For Natasha, the future was less certain: leaving the processing plant for a year meant giving up her job. With limited English and few marketable skills, finding an employer to sponsor her green card application in America would be a challenge. Even if Dasha were accepted to a conservatory, Natasha might have to return to Odessa.

Her second summer at Aspen was even more focused than her first. She spent many days practicing for eight hours, splitting the time between solo repertoire, chamber music, and technical exercises. Everything was more familiar – the setting, the people, the schedule – so she could devote more attention to the piano.

In August, they moved from Aspen to New York City. They lived on the eleventh floor of a doorman building on the Upper West Side. It was close to the Professional Children's School (PCS) and Juilliard so Dasha could walk everywhere easily. Designed for teenagers with active professional lives, the Professional Children's School individualizes each student's schedule so that it's flexible enough to accommodate their other endeavors. Dasha met tennis players, ballerinas, actors, models, and other classical musicians at PCS. She went to school from 8 A.M. to noon each day, then spent the afternoon and evening practicing at her apartment or at Juilliard. On Saturdays, she went to the all-day Pre-College program at Juilliard to play chamber music, study music theory and history, and practice.

New York was noisier and more crowded than Odessa. The sounds of traffic and sirens never stopped. There was also the difficulty of navigating various exchanges and encounters in English. Dasha almost always translated for Natasha, who had trouble speaking more than a few simple words. One of the hardest adjustments was the difference in food. In Odessa, a slice of bread was practically an entire meal. But in New York, most of the bread at the supermarket was thin and sugary and not filling. Tomatoes in Odessa were so fresh you could smell them from across the room. Fruits and vegetables in New York had been shipped in from other countries or states and weren't fresh at all.

Natasha spent her days shopping, cooking, watching Ukrainian TV on the internet, and listening to Dasha practice. On Sundays she and Dasha sometimes took the subway to the Brighton Beach neighborhood of Brooklyn to eat Russian food and speak a familiar language.

Dasha still practiced six to eight hours a day. For her conservatory auditions she was required to prepare music from the Baroque, Classical, Romantic, and Modern periods. She would also be tested on music theory and history. She was meticulous in her preparation. "I highlighted every voice of the Bach fugue in a different color – four colors for four voices," Dasha said. "Then on YouTube I watched performances by Richter, Horowitz, and other pianists I like." During breaks from practicing she instant-messaged her friends from Ukraine, gossiping about mutual acquaintances and answering their endless questions about America: What was the price of a pound of beef? Was New York City full of gangsters, like in the movies?

Over three hundred pianists auditioned for only fifteen spots in the piano department at Juilliard. A few weeks before the audition, Dasha gave a recital at Juilliard to practice her audition repertoire. She knew all of the music intimately, but once on stage she struggled: her memory faltered, she forgot the phrasing she practiced, and she rushed through the repertoire faster than she'd planned.

The day of the audition she warmed up at her apartment and then went to Juilliard. She played for the entire piano faculty, some of whom were familiar from classes at pre-college. They didn't hear her full repertoire, but cut her off a few pages into each piece and asked her to play the next movement or piece. She felt good about her performance, but it was hard to know what the professors thought.

The next day a list of thirty names was posted in the Juilliard lobby. These were the students chosen for callbacks. Dasha and a friend raced to search the list: both had advanced. That afternoon the thirty students took a music theory test and played again for the faculty.

A week later, Dan flew to New York, rented a car, and drove Dasha and Natasha to Baltimore for the audition at Peabody. "Before I started playing, I was nervous," said Dasha. "Will I do all the nuances right? But I'm not nervous when I am playing piano." Natasha was wringing her hands with anxiety as Dasha played. Dan wasn't sure how Dasha really felt about the audition. "You're never quite sure what she's really thinking or feeling. It's a Russian thing."

For the next month they waited to hear the results. Finally, a large envelope from Peabody arrived. She'd been accepted. A few weeks later she learned she hadn't made it into Juilliard.

Acceptance to Peabody was bittersweet; Natasha would have to return to Odessa. There was no way to extend her visa, and even if there were, the Levinsons couldn't afford to help support her indefinitely. Dasha and Natasha had been inseparable: they'd shared a bed, a hotplate, and all of their thoughts for most of Dasha's life. Her mother returned to Odessa to look for work, but she and Dasha talked on Skype almost every day

Dasha often felt her journey from Odessa to America was hard to believe. "We couldn't explain why did it happen, it seemed like a dream." But as she thought about it, she was sure that desire and hard work played some role. "Now I think it happened because we wanted it so much."

*Baby Dasha with her mother, Natasha, in Odessa*

*Dasha and Natasha circa 1998*

*Dasha at one of her first piano competitions*

*Dasha and Natasha with Dan and Lynne Levinson*

*Dasha today*

*Happy times at Aspen
Music Festival*

# APPENDIX

## The Story of From the Top

Every rejection letter has the potential to haunt its senders: agents can never know if they just passed on the next blockbuster novel; colleges frequently deny admission to future luminaries; and investors often decline to back companies like Google that would have made them rich. Though *From the Top* is now broadcast on nearly 250 radio stations around the country and is one of National Public Radio's most popular shows, its story also started with rejection.

One of these rejections is a letter from NPR that Gerald Slavet, the show's co-founder and co-executive director, keeps pinned just behind his computer at the *From the Top* office in Boston. "We had an idea, but no money," Jerry said of the show's beginnings. "Corporations laughed at me. No radio stations were interested. PRI [Public Radio International, the show's initial national distributor] said, 'You should start off small.' I was saying, 'I'm almost sixty, I'm not gonna live long enough, I don't have time for normal processes, slow research, that kind of stuff.'"

Jerry has three basic principles he applies to most of his life. "Never take no from anybody, plow forward, and stay true to your mission." The fact that Jerry's mission, for more than a decade, has been *From the Top* might seem somewhat unlikely. "I have no background as a player or listener of classical music. I was struck by the fact that I'd always been intimidated by classical music until I started sitting in on my daughter's youth orchestra rehearsals. For the first time, classical music became much more accessible to me."

Jerry became so involved with his daughter's youth orchestra at New England Conservatory he volunteered to manage the logistics of several international tours and eventually became a member of

New England Conservatory's (NEC) Board of Trustees. That was when he met Jennifer Hurley-Wales, *From the Top*'s co-founder and co-CEO.

In the mid-1990s, Jennifer was NEC's acting Director of External Affairs and had been charged with bringing in new and different community programming for NEC's signature concert hall – Jordan Hall. After a meeting on this topic, Jerry and Jennifer found themselves on the street corner discussing their ideas. "I remember Jennifer saying to me, 'We should do an old-fashioned radio program.' And I thought immediately it should focus on kids."

Jennifer recalls, "The motivation behind the idea for *From the Top* was personal – a need we each felt. I loved classical music but I didn't like the stuffy culture around it. I loved public radio and *A Prairie Home Companion* and the accessibility and communal feeling and fun of that kind of show."

Using NEC's Jordan Hall as a venue and drawing on kids from the conservatory, they made a few pilot episodes with the help of public radio veterans Jon Solins from WGBH, and independent producer Wesley Horner.

When the concept for the program was presented for a focus group of radio station program directors, the response was mixed. "Why on earth would I play a program with a bunch of kids," said one, "when I could play a recording of Yo-Yo Ma instead?"

In a characteristically defiant moment, Jerry returned to the Public Radio Music Director's Conference with a blind listening test asking them to distinguish between the performance of a sensational nine-year-old violinist, Susan Jang from Ada, Michigan, and that of the legendary violinist Gil Shaham. When the radio professionals flunked his quiz, Jerry proved his point.

Eventually, Public Radio International (PRI) came on board as the show's distributor, but additional funding was needed. "We weren't sure where to turn," Jerry recalls. "Then someone said, 'Have you thought about the federal government?' so I cold-called lobbyists and congressmen. Finally, I convinced the right people and we got a colloquy inserted into the congressional record, but we were told it was too late for anything to happen until the next year's budget. That was too long for me to wait. I went to Washington, DC and visited Congressman Joe Moakley. He was from South Boston, a working-class neighborhood, I said, 'Joe, there is nothing in this for me. I'm just a kid from Mattapan (another working-class neighborhood in Boston). I need your help.' We got a half a million dollar grant from the US Department of Education that year."

*From the Top's* pilot programs premiered on radio in early 1999, launching on seventy-seven stations around the country. This was a monumental achievement at the time, as PRI had warned it would take time to build interest, and that the team should focus on debuting on ten to twenty stations to test the market. Never one to back down from a challenge, Jerry, along with veteran radio marketing consultant Sue Schardt, called every station in the system to ask for a chance.

Upon securing a second grant from the U.S. Department of Education, *From the Top* was ready to begin taping its debut season of new programs. The first program, which wouldn't air until the following January, was taped in July, 1999 at Tanglewood in western Massachusetts.

While the show has evolved over the years, Jerry's and Jennifer's vision of its purpose has remained constant. "The idea was to make heroes of these kids the same way we do with our athletes. We have all these young artists that work just as hard or harder than athletes, but if you're a soccer player or a football player you're already the star of the school. Not so for classical music. A lot of the kids are embarrassed to share what they do with their peers. It's crazy. We also try to break stereotypes – we have jocks, rebels, high-achievers, theater kids, nerds – as broad a cross-section as you'll find amongst any group of kids."

Jennifer was motivated by a similar desire. "We were in love with our idea of a live event taped for radio with classical musicians that might actually be fun … even funny … as well as beautiful, inspiring and interesting."

Jerry was the host of the show on the first two pilot episodes. "I loved being host, I could ask questions as a total ignoramus. But we knew the show needed someone else to grow. So I fired myself and we found Chris."

♪ ♪ ♪

Christopher O'Riley grew up in Evanston, one of Chicago's northern suburbs, and started piano lessons at the age of four. Some of his first memories involve listening to recordings of Beethoven symphonies and dancing around, inventing a narrative as he listened. His first teacher was a Hungarian woman named Lilli Simon with a studio of sixty students. She invariably held her annual studio recitals on, "the hottest day of summer," Chris recalled. His first experiences of recitals were mixtures of heat, sweat, boredom, and hours of piano music. Though the recitals were painful, Chris enjoyed piano intensely for the rest of the year. His mind grasped the basic logic and patterns of key signatures and harmonies. When the note middle C was first pointed out to him he remembers it making "an enormous amount of sense."

By the time he'd started middle school he realized "Classical music wasn't winning me any friends. My sister listened to pop and went to the skating rink. I lacked the frame of reference of most kids." So he started listening to music in the Top Forty – Led Zeppelin, the Doors, and other popular music. As he listened, he figured out how to play and harmonize the melodies on the piano. By the time he started high school he'd formed a band with a few other guys. They called themselves Anomia.

Before high school, Chris' practice schedule was dictated more by desire than by parental pressure. "One to two hours would have been a miracle, my practice was very sporadic at first, which was actually a blessing. Had I been too intense at an early age I might have burned out, whereas now I play all day happily."

Just as he started high school his parents divorced. After his mom remarried, they moved to Pittsburgh, where his stepdad had founded the classical music radio station. "It took me a while to like Pittsburgh. I was upset by the move at first, and by having to leave the band I'd started. But there were certain things to appreciate – I still think of Pittsburgh in autumn, the foliage, the cobblestone streets and farmers' markets. I also had a few great jobs in high school that never could have happened elsewhere."

One of the jobs was in a record store, where he worked after school, and spent hours listening to different kinds of music. Through a contact there, he met a blind saxophone player named Eric Kloss, who invited him to sit in with his jazz ensemble at a club called the Stage Door Lounge. Chris played with the group a few times, and when the regular pianist quit, he found himself with a steady gig. They played two or three sets on Friday or Saturday nights, usually finishing well after midnight. "Initially, everything I did was by ear, and I'd never had formal jazz instruction. In high school I started to read through fake books and playing at the Stage Door taught me to really listen and learn from older players."

He was also getting more serious about classical piano. Between his jazz playing, preparation for college auditions, and work at the record store he was doing something musical almost every moment of the day. "I was at home very little, I was either practicing at school, at the record store, or at the club."

As a student at New England Conservatory, which he chose for its Boston location and the freedom to study jazz as well as classical, he took to practicing for hours and hours, often skipping classes and spending entire days at the piano. He had, "no life outside of NEC." In order to get a practice room he had to claim one before 7 A.M. each morning. On days he couldn't find a room he'd play pinball or go to the movies. "I really liked the long hours at the piano. I was responsible for an enormous amount of music – trios, solos, ensembles, accompanying – you develop a 'body clock,' an immediate and internal sense of what it'll take to get a certain piece ready." Russell Sherman, one of his teachers at NEC, helped to develop his interpretive aesthetic. "He was a great reader and speaker, he encouraged rigorous thought at the piano and elsewhere. He wanted his students to develop the rigor of their own interpretive thought."

He skipped so many classes he never received his bachelor's degree, but he did get an Artists Diploma in Solo Performance.

After leaving NEC, Chris won the prestigious Young Concert Artists Award in New York, and was accepted to compete in the Van Cliburn Competition. He didn't find the competition as ruthless and daunting as it's often depicted to be. "There's a certain sink-or-swim quality, but they want you to feel comfortable, they try to make it possible for you to play your best."

Chris was a finalist in the 1981 Van Cliburn Competition, and through the experience he met an agent and began concertizing. As he performed around the country he noticed how many communities were "dying out in their love of classical music." There was a general sense of malaise: presenters were canceling appearances, audiences were sparse. At least part of the problem was what Chris calls "the ritual-museum" aspect of classical music, the etiquette that says interaction – clapping or talking between movements – is forbidden.

He also saw attempts to revitalize the classical music scene. "Some people made their season brochures look like the cover of a harlequin romance; they tried to present concerts as the latest singles' hangout. I was looking for a balance, something that respects the solitary nature of music but harnesses its communal potential. It's not an exclusive art form, but it's been pushed that way."

While living in New York, Chris started attending weekly soirees often attended by people like Andy Warhol and Allen Ginsberg. "I looked up one night and there was Andy Warhol." Another week, he sat next to Allen Ginsberg at dinner. He often played chamber music at the gatherings. "It showed me that the trappings of classical music were immaterial, that connection is possible in any context. It doesn't have to be Carnegie Hall."

♩ ♩ ♩

Jerry knew Chris was an NEC alum, and after he and Jennifer saw a CBS *Sunday Morning* profile of Chris, in which his enthusiasm for classical music was matched by his interest in pop culture, they contacted him about the possibility of hosting *From the Top*. "I was instantly interested when Jerry reached out. Jerry had all kinds of pre-college musicians in mind, and he was letting kids be the emissaries for classical music – it's a very powerful idea."

The show also provided a platform for Chris to introduce audiences to his arrangements of Radiohead and other mainstream bands. "To some people classical musicians doing crossover smacks of opportunism. I don't choose music simply because it's popular or obscure, I play things that interest me. For me there's always been a fine line between obsession and arranging. The pieces I end up doing arrangements of are just the ones that I've been listening to thousands of times. Music I choose to arrange has elements that appeal to classical listeners. There's textural richness, it's not homophonic, monolithic pop."

He also defends crossover playing on the basis of historical precedence. "The fact is this sort of thing has existed for hundreds of years. But in earlier periods there wasn't the same tendency to see versatility or broad interests as a betrayal of so-called high art."

Chris was able to play some of his Radiohead arrangements on *From the Top* as a break piece where some stations did their stations identifications. Soon fans were writing in to learn more about the music he played. "Who is this Mr. Head, and where can I find more of his beautiful music?" one fan wrote.

Chris also enjoyed interacting with the kids during the show and serving as an accompanist for certain pieces. "It felt like a new way to present music, giving these small portraits of the kids through interview and narratives. I take the script for each show and get the major points, but I don't want to just ask questions with blinkers on. I try to stay in the moment and improvise when appropriate. The fact that it sounds conversational has to do with the wealth of information we gather about each kid before the show."

Each musician who appears on *From the Top* goes through extensive interviews with staff so the script for a given show can best reflect the specific personalities of the kids featured. "We take the source material each kid gives us and portray them in the best possible light."

*From the Top*'s method of presenting music in the context of personal narratives and interviews is now increasingly common in the classical music world. "I see the influence everywhere," Chris said. The Van Cliburn Competition now emphasizes the backstories and personalities of its contestants through interviews and short videos, and orchestras around the country have become increasingly interested in combining narrative with performance. In the 2008–2009 season, Chris was a guest conductor at the Columbus Symphony Orchestra. During the concerts, he interviewed various orchestra members on stage about musical and personal topics. "The Columbus Symphony has been to the grave and back and they were looking for a way to renew the audience's connection to the orchestra. So why not interview members of the orchestra? It was very much in the style of *From the Top*."

The organization's influence is also spreading through the work of its Center for the Development of Arts Leaders, a program designed to help *From the Top* alumni, as well as other young musicians around the country, fulfill their potential as leaders and engage with their local communities through their music. "Our ten years of producing *From the Top* events and broadcasts have taught us that young people can make an important impact on the world by sharing who they are and what they love to do," said Jerry.

Now a student at Berklee College of Music, Clifton Williams is a part of the Center for the Development of Arts Leaders' pilot year in Boston, which has paired twenty young musicians with five community partners for a year-long service project using music as a vehicle for change.

Jerry and Jennifer are particularly passionate about providing access to music and training to people of all backgrounds. "The Jack Kent Cooke Foundation has been a great partner with *From the Top*. Together we've been able to help a lot of kids pursue their musical training, despite financial limitations." Since their partnership began in 2005, The Jack Kent Cooke Foundation has awarded nearly 150 scholarships to *From the Top* musicians with financial need. Each scholarship is a $10,000 award that helps students pay for tuition, music lessons or new instruments. Dasha Bukhartseva and Clifton Williams were both recipients of this scholarship.

With hundreds of alumni around the country, many veterans of the show are now in a position to give back as performers and teachers. "I run into them everywhere," Chris said of the show's alumni. "They are at festivals, concerts, they come back for shows."

While the show has a different impact on each participant, many young musicians find it has helped them realize music's power to bring people together. Jerry recalls, "An alum said to us, 'Most shows are just like, come and play and leave, but that's what I love about *From the Top*. It's not like a regularly produced show. You all come together and have this amazing time making the show and then feel so proud when you hear or see it. It's not just an accomplishment, but it's like you have a whole new set of friends.'"

# About the Author

Nick Romeo has written program notes and profiles for Carnegie Hall. His journalism regularly appears in magazines around the country. He lives in Boulder, Colorado.

Each musician profiled in this book has appeared on NPR's *From the Top*. To listen to their radio shows and see videos and photos, please visit www.fromthetop.org/driven.

Proof

Made in the USA
Charleston, SC
21 July 2011